"Very clear and precise. A layman can take thi[s] amounts of mistakes and actually make good movi[e]..."

— Alan Siegel, California Teacher of the Year (2005), teaches at nationally recognized, award-winning Carle High School

"You've written a real nuts and bolts, straightforward primer (and more) for anyone who wants to learn about the DV camera and how to use it. The reader can use *Digital Video Secrets* to shore up weaknesses and bolster strengths. It's chock full of useful information. I'm writing a script at the moment and Tony Levelle's book is already widening my options for setups as I come into each scene."

— Christopher Keane, author of *Romancing the A List: How to Write the Script the Big Stars Want to Make*

"Tony Levelle has put between two covers everything you need to know about the best and brightest ways to use your digital camera, regardless of what you're shooting — from wedding videos to the next big ground-breaking low-budget sensation."

— John Gaspard, author of *Digital Filmmaking 101, Fast, Cheap and Under Control* and *Fast, Cheap and Written That Way*

"I only wish this book had been available years ago. The author illustrates his points with personal stories and he cuts to the chase on matters technical — which he seems to know and understand in depth. His section on camera angles is a 'must read' for anyone thinking about picking up a camera. I have no doubt that this book will find itself dirty and dog-eared in many a set bag of working filmmakers in the future — including myself."

— Richard La Motte, independent filmmaker, author of *Costume Design 101*

"As someone who has been shooting digitally since the early days of 1997, after even the most cursory read I know that *Digital Video Secrets* is a volume that no beginning digital filmmaker should be without."

— Scott Essman, director of the acclaimed digital documentary *A Tribute to John Chambers*

[DIGITAL VIDEO]
[S E C R E T S]

What the Pros Know and the Manuals Don't Tell You

Tony Levelle

MICHAEL WIESE PRODUCTIONS

Published by Michael Wiese Productions

3940 Laurel Canyon Blvd. – Suite 1111

Studio City, CA 91604

(818) 379-8799, (818) 986-3408 (FAX).

mw@mwp.com

www.mwp.com

Cover design by Kevin Capizzi

Interior design by William Morosi

Copyedited by Paul Norlen

Printed by McNaughton & Gunn

Manufactured in the United States of America

Library of Congress Cataloging-in-Publication Data

Levelle, Tony, 1944-

Digital video secrets / Tony Levelle.

   p. cm.

Includes bibliographical references and index.

ISBN 978-1-932907-47-6 (alk. paper)

1. Digital video. I. Title.

TK6680.5.L48 2008

778.59--dc22

                     2008022849

TABLE OF CONTENTS

ACKNOWLEDGMENTS

I wish to express my deep appreciation to the people who encouraged and supported me during the writing of this book.

Thanks to Marsha, for her good humor, friendship and love. My family was constantly supportive, but especially Pete, whose cheerful friendship got me through some tough spots.

Michael Wiese and Ken Lee were steadfastly supportive. Michael stood behind me through a string of extraordinary difficulties that no one could have anticipated when work began on *Producing with Passion* and *Digital Video Secrets*.

An extraordinary group of people gave advice, read early drafts, and took me out for coffee when I needed it. Thanks to Jim Jackson, Tom and Gail Marquette, Gloria Hovde, Dianna Brooks, David L. Brown, Jack Barker, and Philip Rhodes.

Barbara Clark volunteered to model for the photographs at the last minute. She was unfailingly cheerful, enthusiastic and a delight to work with. I am deeply indebted to her.

Alan Siegel and his video production class at Carle High School in Lower Lake, California read early drafts, and gave me valuable feedback. Thanks to Ben Hopper, Jared Mills, Aaron Moore, Cy Matthew Passley, and Kurtis Pecchenino.

Jon and Marcella Jost were unfailingly generous in answering questions and sharing their insights and knowledge of filmmaking in general and producing and editing digital video in particular.

Thanks to Cinequest *www.cinequest.org*. Cinequest produces the annual Cinequest Film Festival and the Cinequest Distribution Label.

Finally, thanks to Dorothy and Jim Fadiman, for their unfailing friendship and loving guidance in filmmaking, writing, and creativity.

Any mistakes and omissions in this book are mine, and only mine.

INTRODUCTION

I want you to capture extraordinary images and create great videos.

Whether you want to make a feature film, family video, or capture the first steps of your new son or daughter, I want you to be successful!

None of the things in this book are really secret. They are the things that "everyone knows," but nobody tells you. I've been bitten by every one of these "secrets." Each one of them cost me precious time, money and effort to learn.

I wrote this book because, after running a small local film festival for nearly ten years, and being a juror at an international film festival, I realized that I wasn't alone in being "bitten."

When I researched this book, I tested all sorts of cameras, from a $149 Flip camera with one button ("Record") to a $3,000 Panasonic prosumer camera with dozens of buttons and menus. I learned that *everyone has the same problems.* Whether you are shooting with a toy video camera or a prosumer camera, you have to solve these problems.

This book will show you how to:
- Shoot fluently and confidently
- Shoot visually pleasing and compelling images
- Record clear and vivid sound
- Shoot footage that has continuity from shot to shot
- Shoot footage that is editable
- Choose the best camera for you

Go to www.tonylevelle.com for more information and free *Digital Video Secrets* extras.

Let's start!

QUICK START

Make sure you have everything you need

1. Camera, two fully charged batteries and battery charger.
2. Blank media.
   Depending on the type of storage your camcorder uses, make sure that you have either: two tapes, two flash-memory cards or two DVDs. If your camera uses a hard disk, check to see that you have adequate storage space on the disk.
3. Tripod.
4. Microphones including cables, and fresh batteries for the microphone (if your microphone uses them), and a wind screen.
5. Headphones.
6. Camera manual.

Set up the camera

1. If your camera has a diopter adjustment, adjust it for your eyes.
2. Clean the lens. On these small cameras, every speck of dust will show up on the final image.
3. Decide if you are going to shoot "full auto" mode or "manual mode."
   - Shoot auto mode when you have to shoot quickly, or don't yet understand the camera controls.
   - Shoot manual mode when you have time to set up the camera and want the best possible image.

If you decide to shoot auto mode

1. Turn ON: auto focus, auto exposure, auto white balance and automatic gain control (AGC).
   - Many camcorders have a single button that will engage full auto operation. It may be called something like "Easy" or "Auto."

- Use a tripod whenever possible.
- When shooting people, open the lens wide and get close to the person.
- Keep your subject in the middle of the frame.
- Keep the distance between the subject and the camcorder about the same while you are recording. (If the distance changes, the image will go out of focus momentarily while the camera's auto-focus circuits "hunt" for new focus.)

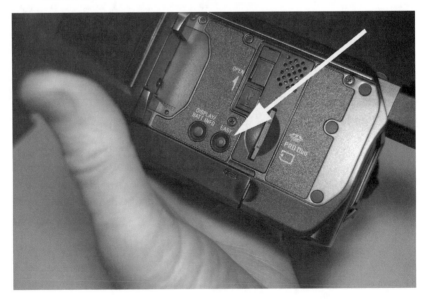

If you decide to shoot manual mode

Not all cameras will have all of these settings. (Settings are explained in chapter 9, Choosing Camera Settings.)

1. Format to HD or SD.
2. Screen ratio to 16x9 or 4x3.
3. Frame rate. (NTSC=60. PAL= 50. Film look=24.)
4. Shutter in manual mode (auto iris OFF)
5. Shutter speed to normal (NTSC=1/60, PAL=1/50, 24-frame film look= 1/48)
6. Focus in manual mode (auto focus OFF)
7. ND filter OFF
8. Audio gain control OFF (AGC OFF)
9. Audio to 16-bit 48 KHz
10. Video gain OFF or ZERO
11. White balance to manual

Shoot a short test

1. Connect the microphones and headphones.
2. Listen to the audio over the headphones.
3. Shoot a short test.
4. Play the test back on a monitor or TV. Compare the picture on the monitor or television to the picture on the LCD. Turn the LCD brightness down until it matches the image on the monitor or TV. Otherwise, the LCD image will mislead you when you are in the field.

CHAPTER 1

SHOOTING FLUENTLY AND CONFIDENTLY

Get to know your camera

Trying to shoot a street scene in the rain is a little like giving a piano recital in the shower.

It is December and I am in Portland, Oregon. Today's weather is the same as yesterday's: wet, cold and windy under a dark morning sky.

I am crouched behind a parked car on Mississippi Avenue. Leaning out a bit, I focus a VX2100 camera on the oncoming traffic. Seven street-cleaning trucks approach in line. Lumbering down the narrow street, throwing white sprays of water from their wheels, they are a perfect visual metaphor for a scene I want to shoot.

As the third truck passes, my viewfinder goes white and I am drenched in ice-cold water. The driver—bored or maybe not liking his picture taken—flipped on the truck's street washing spray as he passed.

I have come to Portland for a week to work with filmmaker Jon Jost. Jost is a slender, charismatic man who has been making feature films for nearly thirty years. The credits on his film usually read: writer, director, producer, editor: Jon Jost. He is a genius at keeping things simple, and doing everything himself.

Although he shot in film for nearly twenty years—16mm and 35mm Panavision—he was an early convert to digital video and decided in 1996 to shoot only on DV.

Of his twenty-something features; *All the Vermeers in New York* is my favorite. Shot in 35mm, without lights, it is a beautifully made, subtle character study.

Jost is in Portland for a few months to prepare for his next feature film. While here, he has agreed to give me a crash course in digital video shooting. The day after I arrived, he learned that one of his recent films had been accepted for the Rotterdam film festival.

In his apartment he and his wife Marcella are working furiously. They are doing last-minute edits and preparing a new digital copy of his film for Rotterdam. Between work sessions, Jon gave me a "mini workshop" on shooting digital video. The exercises that follow are drawn from the formal Digital Video workshops he teaches every year.

SECRET 1: DON'T BE AFRAID OF THE CAMERA

One of the biggest secrets about shooting well is simply to be comfortable with your camera.

The best way to become comfortable with any camera is to take the camera out, turn it on and play with it.

Shoot some footage and see what happens. For now, don't worry about what the image looks like. As filmmaker Jon Jost tells his students in his Digital Video workshops, "Just make a mess!"

What you need for this exercise:
- Camcorder with a fully charged battery
- Blank media. Depending on your camera, the media may be a tape, flash memory chip, DVD, or hard disk
- Camcorder operating manual
- Computer with video editing software

1. Find a comfortable spot where you won't be disturbed. You can do this in your kitchen, your front yard, or a local park.
2. Start recording.

3. Push all the buttons. Try every control on the camera. Learn how to interpret every word and icon on the LCD.
4. Keep going until you have about fifteen minutes of footage.
5. Dump the footage into your computer and make a three-minute movie of the most visually interesting shots.
6. Give your three-minute movie a title and save it to a DVD or CD.
7. Post your movie online.

Posting your movies online

After each exercise, you might want to post your films online. There are several reasons why this is a good idea, one of which is that it is an excellent way to develop the habit of finishing every project that you shoot.

YouTube accounts are free at *www.youtube.com* .

You can see my own videos of each exercise (and find many free *Digital Video Secrets* extras) at *www.tonylevelle.com*.

SECRET 2: LEARN TO "SEE" WITH THE CAMERA

When you look at a scene, develop the habit looking at it through the camera. Use the camera as a lens, through which you observe the world. When you look at a scene with your eyes, you see all sorts of things on the periphery of your vision. The camera doesn't see any of this. The camera only sees what is within the frame.

When you practice seeing the world through the camera, you soon develop a sense of framing, composition and balance. Learning to see with the camera is the first step toward shooting truly compelling images.

What you need for this exercise:
- Camcorder with a fully charged battery
- Blank media
- Tripod or camera support.
- Computer with video editing software
- Camcorder operating manual

1. Find a visually interesting spot within a five-minute walk of your home. Look for a spot where you can see movement—traffic, people walking, waves crashing on a shore, clouds moving across the sky—anything.
2. Sit down, and turn on the camera. Look at the scene on the LCD. Move the camera, and play with the zoom until you find an interesting scene.
3. Record the scene. Hold the camera on the scene for at least one minute. The first thing you will notice is how hard it is to let the camera record for even a single minute. We're all so conditioned to quick cuts and jumps on television and in the movies, that there's a constant temptation to move the camera to something else. Watch the scene in the camcorder viewfinder or LCD as you record it. Don't look up.

4. Repeat five times, with five different scenes.
5. Dump the resulting footage into your computer and carefully examine the footage.
6. Assemble a two- or three-minute movie from the most visually interesting elements of the footage.
7. Give your movie a title and save it to DVD or CD. Write the date, time, and the name of the movie on the DVD or CD.
8. Post your movie online.

SECRET 3: LEARN TO SHOOT INTUITIVELY

Closely connected to learning to "see" with the camera is the ability to shoot intuitively and spontaneously.

Some of the world's greatest photographs were only captured because the photographer had the ability to shoot intuitively and quickly.

What you need for this exercise:
- Camcorder with a fully charged battery
- Blank media
- Computer with video editing software

1. Take your camcorder, and go for a walk. Don't make a big deal of it; just go somewhere close by, maybe somewhere that you see every day. As you walk, look at your environment. When you see something that interests you—for no reason other than it interests you—stop and record it, no matter how little sense it makes. Shoot at least thirty seconds of footage each time you turn on the camera. (Thirty seconds gives you enough footage so you can edit it easily.)
2. Continue until you have five to seven minutes of footage.
3. Dump the footage into your computer.
4. Assemble a one to three-minute movie from the most interesting shots.
5. Give the movie a title and save it to CD or DVD.
6. Post the movie online.

SECRET 4: LEARN TO OPERATE YOUR CAMERA BY TOUCH

Being able to turn on the camera and shoot without looking at the camera allows you to shoot verite or to blend into the environment in a way that you couldn't if you had to stop, open the viewfinder or LCD, focus and frame the image.

The ability to shoot "from the hip" is a good way to get an unexpected angle on a scene. You can often capture very interesting and revealing footage using this technique.

This skill is closely associated with the other steps in shooting fluently.

- What you need for this exercise:
- Camcorder with a fully charged battery

- Blank media
- Camcorder operating manual
- Computer with video editing software

1. Find an interesting place, someplace where you can tape safely and unobtrusively. It may be a park, a city street, or even your own back yard.
2. Use the viewfinder or LCD to frame a scene. Adjust the camcorder's zoom, focus, shutter, iris and white balance.
3. Close the LCD, and hold the camera at waist level. Point the camera toward the scene.
4. Record the scene for a minute or longer. Do not peek at the viewfinder or LCD while you are recording.
5. Repeat five times in different locations.
6. Dump the footage into your computer.
7. Select the most interesting footage and assemble a two to three-minute movie.
8. Give your movie a title and save it to CD or DVD.
9. Post your movie online.

SECRET 5: LEARN TO SHOOT WITH BOTH EYES OPEN

When you are shooting on location, learn to shoot with both eyes open. This is useful if you are doing what is called "shooting verite." When you shoot verite, you try to be like a "fly on the wall." You observe and film, without being a part of the scene.

Shooting with both eyes open is also useful if you need to walk while you are recording. When you are concentrating on the image in your viewfinder, it's amazingly easy to do something dangerous—like accidentally stepping into a swimming pool. When you shoot with both eyes open, you remain aware of the immediate environment as you shoot.

It's a little bit like learning to rub your head while patting your stomach. You can learn it with practice!

What you need for this exercise:
- Camcorder with a fully charged battery
- Blank media
- Computer with video editing software

1. Find a safe, unobstructed place where you can walk about as you film. This may be in your own home or back yard.
2. With one eye on the viewfinder, and the other eye open, walk about the location. Hold the camera as steady as possible, and keep the viewfinder at your eye. Don't lower the camcorder until you finish all five shots in this exercise.

3. Frame as you go. When you see something interesting, stop and record thirty seconds of footage.
4. When you have five minutes of footage, stop.
5. Dump the footage into your NLE, and edit the most interesting scenes into a one to two-minute movie.
6. Give your movie a title and save it on a CD or DVD.
7. Post your movie online.

SECRET 6: SHOOT A MOVIE WITH A UNIFYING THEME

For this exercise, you will shoot a series of images with a unifying theme.

Shooting a series of shots with a unifying theme will develop your ability to create visual transitions between shots, and establish continuity between scenes.

This exercise develops visual literacy. As you assemble movies based on a unifying theme, you will become aware of the visual power of certain images, colors, and compositions.

What you need for this exercise:
- Camcorder with fully charged batteries
- Blank media
- Tripod or other camera support
- Computer with video editing software

1. Shoot a series of shots with a unifying theme. The unifying theme might be subject, color, movement... anything that appeals to you, as long as there is a visual relationship between one shot and the next.
2. Record at least twenty seconds on each shot.
3. Continue until you have five minutes of footage.
4. When you have five minutes of footage dump it into your computer and edit it down to a two to three-minute movie of the most visually interesting scenes.
5. Give your movie a title and save it to DVD or CD.
6. Post your movie online.

SECRET 7: SHOOT A MOVIE A DAY FOR SIXTY DAYS

One of the most useful things you can do to become fluent with your camera is to shoot and edit a five-minute movie every day for sixty days. You can edit the movie "in camera" or in your computer. When you edit "in camera" plan each shot so that it will transition visually to the next.

Keep your shots simple. If you make them too complicated, you may find it difficult to shoot every day. Aim for completing a simple movie, every day.

Remember: "Done is good!"

Shoot intuitively. Do not over-plan. Soon you will begin to see a pattern in your movies. It will be a pattern of your own interests and enthusiasms. This pattern may reveal the kind of moviemaking that interests you deeply, and which you might do well.

At the end of sixty days you will probably have one or two good little movies.

What you need for this exercise:
- Camcorder with a fully charged battery
- Blank media
- Notebook and pencil
- Camcorder operating manual
- Computer with video editing software

1. At the beginning of each day's shoot, write down the date and subject of the day's footage.
2. Film this page as the first shot of the day.
3. Shoot ten to fifteen minutes of footage in as many or as few scenes as you like. Don't worry about story, image quality, tripods, filters, light, white balance or anything else. Focus on getting something done each day, rather than getting it "right." Remember, "Done is good!"
4. In your computer, edit the most interesting chunks into a five-minute movie.
5. Repeat for sixty days.

CHAPTER 2

WATCHING FILMS MADE BY OTHERS

We all have similar problems when it comes to filmmaking

Secret 8: *Watch other films made on DV and HDV*
A list of award-winning DV films

I was a film festival juror

Shortly after finishing *Producing with Passion*, a book on documentary filmmaking, I got a call from Cinequest Film Festival. Would I be interested in being a juror at an upcoming Cinequest?

Three weeks later I found myself in an all expenses paid hotel in San Jose, California. For the next five days, my fellow jurors and I watched films from all over the world. Many of the films were shot on digital video, and all of them were works of passion and love.

The people who made these films had sacrificed their money, time, and occasionally their health to get through the year or more that it takes to make a feature film.

If the films I saw taught me anything, they taught me that it is possible to make a serious movie with a digital video camera and get it into a major film festival.

Of course this doesn't include the money you might have to raise, the year or so of your life, and the nights when you wake up at 1:30 AM, with your guts in a knot because you have no idea how you are going to get a location. Or where you'll find a leading man to replace the actor who just went into the hospital, or how you are going to pay next month's rent.

Of course, there are other options. Instead of making an independent film for a year, you could spend a year living in the city, paying rent, and working at a job. At the end of such a year, most people would have absolutely nothing to show for the year. At the very least these filmmakers had something to show for their year: a finished film, new skills, and a chance to hang out at film festivals.

Watching 100 films

After a few days of watching films, I began to realize how important it is that every part of a film must work! Any part that is weak damages the whole film.

It doesn't matter where the problem is, whether it's story, sound, acting, directing, camera work—everything has to work before you have a good film. There are no shortcuts.

I was struck by the fact that jurors tended to agree on the major elements of a film. If the sound was weak, everyone would notice it. If the story was weak, everyone would notice it. This was true for every film.

This taught me two things. 1) Every filmmaker faces similar problems. 2) Every independent film can be a lesson to other filmmakers in how to solve these problems.

SECRET 8: WATCH OTHER FILMS MADE ON DV AND HDV

One of the fastest ways to improve your filmmaking — besides shooting lots of films — is to watch a lot of film.

A list of award-winning DV films

Choosing films for the following list was difficult. In the last few years, literally thousands of people have made films with digital video cameras. I finally decided to look for films that were made with digital video cameras, and which had either won awards or gotten theatrical release. I also added several that I'd heard other filmmakers mention.

There are plenty of great films that are not on this list.

A word about theatrical release

While looking for films to add to this list, I tended to favor those films that had gotten a theatrical release, even though many excellent films never get theatrical release. Increasingly, a theatrical release is little more than advertising for future DVD sales.

DVDs are a tremendous opportunity for independent filmmakers. Independent films can exist forever on DVD, either through direct sales from the filmmaker's website or through online rentals from companies like Netflix.

Nearly all the movies on the list below are available on Netflix.

This list of films is arranged alphabetically, by film title.

Title	Year	Director	Cinematographer	Camera(s)
24 Hour Party People	2002	Michael Winterbottom	Robby Müller	Sony DSR-PD150
28 Days Later...	2002	Danny Boyle	Anthony Dod Mantle	Canon XL-1S with some 35mm and 8mm film.
6 Easy Pieces	2000	Jon Jost	Jon Jost	Sony DCR-VX1000
9 Songs	2004	Michael Winterbottom	Marcel Zyskind	Panasonic AG-DVX100A / Sony DSR-PD150
A Scanner Darkly	2006	Richard Linklater	Shane F. Kelly	Panasonic AG-DVX100
An Inconvenient Truth	2006	Davis Guggenheim	Davis Guggenheim, Bob Richman	JVC GY-HD100U with Sony HDC-F950 and Sony HDV Camera
Bamboozled	2000	Spike Lee	Ellen Kuras	Sony DCR-TRV900 / Sony DCR-VX1000
Chelsea Walls	2001	Ethan Hawke	Tom Richmond	Sony DSR-PD100 (PAL)
Chuck and Buck	2000	Miguel Arteta	Chuy Chavez	Sony DCR-VX1000
Dancer in the Dark	2000	Lars von Trier	Robby Müller	Sony DSR-1P, Sony DSR-PD100P, Sony DSR-PD150, Sony DXC-D30WSP
Deliver Us from Evil	2006	Amy Berg	Jacob Kusk, Jens Schlosser	Sony HVR-Z1
Dogville	2003	Lars von Trier	Anthony Dod Mantle	Sony DSR-PD150P and Sony HDW-F900.
Erleuchtung garantiert (Enlightenment guaranteed)	2000	Doris Dörrie	Hans Karl Hu	Sony DCR-TRV900 (PAL)
Everything Put Together	2001	Marc Forster	Roberto Schaefer	Sony DCR-VX1000

Title	Year	Director	Cinematographer	Camera(s)
Favela Rising	2005	Matt Mochary Jeff Zimbalist	Kelly Mark Green Matt Mochary Jeff Zimbalist	Panasonic AG-DVX100
Final	2001	Campbell Scott	Dan Gillham	Canon XL-1 (PAL)
Full Frontal	2002	Steven Soderbergh	Peter Andrews	Canon XL-1S
Hotel	2001	Mike Figgis	Patrick Alexander Stewart	Sony PD 100 & PD150 PAL
Inland Empire	2006	David Lynch	Odd-Geir Sæther	Sony DSR-PD150
Iraq in Fragments	2006	James Longley	James Longley	Panasonic AG-DVX100
Jackass	2002	Jeff Tremaine	Dimitry Elyashkevich	Canon GL-1 Canon XL-1 Sony DCR-VX1000 Sony DCR-VX2000 Sony DSR-PD150
Keep the River on Your Right	2000	David Shapiro Laurie Shapiro	Jonathan Kovel	Canon XL-1
Land of Plenty	2004	Wim Wenders	Franz Lustig	Panasonic AG-DVX100
Landspeed: CKY	1999	Bam Margera	Ryan Gee, Bam Margera	Sony DCR-VX1000
Lonesome Jim	2005	Steve Buscemi	Phil Parmet	Panasonic AG-DVX100
Mad Hot Ballroom	2005	Marilyn Agrelo	Claudia Raschke	Panasonic AG-DVX100
Manic	2001	Jordan Melamed	Nick Hay	Sony DSR-PD150
Meeting People Is Easy	1998	Grant Gee	Grant Gee	Sony PC7 PAL
Murderball	2005	Henry Alex Rubin Dana Adam Shapiro	Henry Alex Rubin	Panasonic AG-DVX100A
My Little Eye	2002	Marc Evans,	Hubert Taczanowski	Sony DSR-PD150P
November	2004	Greg Harrison	Nancy Schreiber	Panasonic AG-DVX100A
One Life Stand	2000	May Miles Thomas	May Miles Thomas	Sony VX1000E PAL
Open Water	2003	Chris Kentis	Chris Kentis Laura Lau	Sony DCR-VX2000 Sony DSR-PD150
Personal Velocity: Three Portraits	2002	Rebecca Miller	Ellen Kuras	Sony DSR-PD150P and Sony HDCAM Cameras
Pieces of April	2003	Peter Hedges	Tami Reiker	Sony DSR-PD150
Pinero	2001	Leon Ichaso Claudio Chea		Canon XL-1
Promised Land	2004	Amos Gitai	Caroline Champetier	Panasonic AG-DVX100
Rock School	2005	Don Argott	Don Argott	Panasonic AG-DVX100A

Title	Year	Director	Cinematographer	Camera(s)
Sacred Sites of the Dalai Lamas	2007	Michael Wiese	Michael Wiese	Sony PD150
Saltmen of Tibet	1997	Ulrike Koch	Pio Corradi	Sony VX1000E PAL
Sketches of Frank Gehry	2005	Sydney Pollack	Marcus Birsel Ultan Guilfoyle Sydney Pollack Claudio Rocha George Tiffin	Canon GL-2
Slacker	1991	Richard Linklater	Lee Daniel	Fisher-Price PXL 2000 "PixelVision" (bar scene)
Some Body	2001	Henry Barrial	Geoffrey Pepos	Canon XL1
Spellbound	2002	Jeffrey Blitz	Jeffrey Blitz	Canon XL-1
Startup.com	2001	Chris Hegedus Jehane Noujaim	Jehane Noujaim	Canon XL-1 Sony DSR-PD100
Storm of Emotions				
Super Size Me	2004	Morgan Spurlock	Scott Ambrozy	Sony DSR-PD150
Surfing for Life	1999	David L. Brown Roy Earnest	David L. Brown	Canon XL-1
Tape	2001	Richard Linklater	Maryse Alberti	Sony DSR-PD100
The Ballad of Ramblin' Jack	2001	Aiyana Elliott	Aiyana Elliott	Sony VX1000 and Hi-8 camera
The Book of Life	1998	Hal Hartley	Jim Denault	Sony DCR-VX1000
The Celebration	1998	Thomas Vinterberg	Anthony Dod Mantle	Sony PC7 PAL
The Chateau	2001	Jesse Peretz	Tom Richmond	Sony TRV 900 PAL
The Cruise	1998	Bennett Miller	Bennett Miller	Sony VX1000
The Idiots	1998	Lars von Trier	Casper Holm Jesper Jargil Kristoffer Nyholm Lars von Trier	Sony VX1000 PAL
The King Is Alive	2000	Kristian Levring	Jens Schlosser	Sony PD 100 PAL
The Road to Guantanamo	2006	Michael Winterbottom, Mat Whitecross	Marcel Zyskind	Panasonic AG-DVX100A
The War Tapes	2006	Deborah Scranton	Peter Ciardelli P.H. O'Brien	Sony VCR 105, 109, and 350. Stateside interviews on Sony DVCAM and Panasonic DV camcorders.
The Wild Dogs	2002	Thom Fitzgerald	Tom Harting	Sony PD150
Waking Life	2001	Richard Linklater	Richard Linklater Tommy Pallotta	Sony DCR-TRV900

CHAPTER 3

COMPOSING POWERFUL, COMPELLING IMAGES

*Composition is the key
to achieving powerful images*

When I was in film school I decided to shoot my student film in 16mm film. At midnight. On location. In downtown San Jose. Thus violating at least four rules of sane filmmaking.

The heart of this complicated, hard to stage, student film was the robbery of a convenience store. I found a convenience store in a working-class neighborhood of San Jose, coordinated the staged "robbery" with the police department, auditioned actors, lined up a crew, and even rented a gun from a company that specialized in supplying weapons to film companies.

The night we filmed, everything went as planned, except for a fight in the parking lot. (The police broke it up. We kept going.) The shoot was strenuous, and exhilarating.

I slept late the next day. When I returned to school that afternoon, I met the kindly gray-haired man who taught the lighting course. He smiled and asked me, "Did you get pretty pictures?"

A few days later, we got the negatives back.

The images were, indeed, pretty. But they weren't compelling or powerful. Without realizing it, I'd shot nearly every image from eye level. The overall effect was bland and indifferent.

All my work, money and time were wasted because I didn't understand the power of camera placement (where the camera is placed in relation to the scene) and composition (how the image is composed in the viewfinder). I was so involved in the mechanics of staging the scene, and getting everything technically perfect that I overlooked composition.

I suddenly realized why the kindly film teacher was smiling. He *knew* I would be so overwhelmed by the challenges of setting up the complicated shoot that I would—just as hundreds of film students before me—overlook composition.

As a digital video filmmaker with a small crew and a smaller budget, you may be in danger of falling into the same trap.

A properly composed image will evoke an emotional response in the audience. A properly composed image is more than pretty. It is compelling.

Filmmakers have been evolving a visual language of film for over a hundred years. Mastery of this visual language probably takes as much time and effort as it takes to learn a spoken language like French or Chinese. Just as a spoken language can be learned, visual language can be learned. Some people learn it easier than others. These fortunate people understand and "speak" the visual language of film easily and fluently.

This chapter is not for them. This chapter is for the rest of us.

Here are a few elementary rules of composition that you can use to improve your shots. With this introduction and much hard work, you too may one day create compelling images, consistently and fluently.

SECRET 9: GET THE FOUR BASIC SHOTS

For every scene you shoot, try to get four basic shots: Establishing Shot, Long Shot, Medium Shot and Close Up.

If you use these four basic shots on every scene, you will get 80% of all the coverage you need. Coverage is the word for getting all the shots required to edit the footage into a workable scene. The word is often used as a noun, as in "Did you get coverage?"

Establishing Shot (ES)

An establishing shot shows where the scene is taking place. Establishing shots are often used to open and close a scene.

Long Shot (LS)

Long shots show the audience the actor's body language and the environment around the actor. Beginning filmmakers often forget to shoot long shots because they are not thinking of getting all the shots they need to edit the scene.

Medium Shot (MS)

Medium shots are often neutral, uninvolved shots. The subject (person) in the shot is being observed, but not closely.

The normal sequence is to begin an interview or scene with a medium shot. As the intensity of the scene slowly builds, the camera moves closer and closer. This transition can be so slow the audience isn't consciously aware of it, or it can be an abrupt transition from MS to CU.

Close Up (CU)

Close-ups are how the audience shares what an actor or interviewee is feeling. This means that you have to get the camera so close that the person's face fills the screen. People avoid shooting close-ups because it's uncomfortable to get the camera in close and record people's intimate facial expressions. This reluctance is so ingrained in our culture that we have a phrase for it. It's called "getting in people's faces."

The viewer, however, needs and wants you to get in people's faces.

Every culture has strong taboos about personal space and how close you can get to someone. Before you get physically close to someone, make sure you have their permission.

SECRET 10: USE THE FIVE BASIC CAMERA ANGLES

The "camera angle" (where the camera is placed) makes a huge difference in how the audience reacts to footage. Different camera angles will evoke different emotional reactions from the audience. This is the reason why political ads often place the camera slightly below the politician, looking up. The politician is literally shown as someone the audience should "look up to."

As you watch films and advertisements, pay attention to the camera angle. Try to see what reaction the filmmaker is trying to get from the audience.

Here are seven angles to consider using when you shoot your scenes:

Looking-down

When you place the camera above and looking down on a person or scene, the viewer has the emotional effect of "looking down" on the scene. When used with a character, it subtly makes the audience feel superior to the character, or it suggests someone who is beaten down, submissive or powerless. This angle is often used to suggest that the actor or person being filmed is a victim or a contemptible character. Someone you "look down on."

Looking-up

If the camera is below a person and looking up, the image suggests an overpowering being—someone you "look up to." This angle is commonly used to make political leaders appear authoritarian and decisive. Watch for this one in political advertisements.

Straight-on

If the camera is looking straight on at the person, the person appears "equal" to the viewer. This angle is commonly used in infomercials to make the narrator appear to be a person who is honest and "straightforward."

Dutch angle

A Dutch angle is created by simply tilting the camera sideways. When you tilt the camera slightly, you suggest that things are "out of order" or "skewed." (You see this angle a lot in horror movies.)

Dutch angle is also used subtly—and sometimes not so subtly—by political operatives who want to suggest that an opposing political candidate is untrustworthy or out-of-control.

Angle plus angle

Shooting at an angle to the subject, while tilting up or down is called an angle plus angle shot. This is a simple technique that you can use to give visual interest to otherwise boring shots. When on buildings it can add depth and indicate volume.

SECRET 11: USE BOTH OBJECTIVE AND SUBJECTIVE VIEWS

When you think about how you want to shoot a scene, ask yourself whether you want the audience to see the action through the character's eyes or whether you want them to watch the action from one side.

Objective view

Objective angle shows the scene to the audience as if they were standing off to one side and watching. This view has the effect of giving the audience information without pulling them into the scene emotionally.

Subjective view

Subjective angle is the view as seen by a character in a scene. This angle has the effect of pulling the audience into the scene emotionally and building empathy with a character.

SECRET 12: **COMPOSE ON THE RULE OF THIRDS**

The rule of thirds is a centuries-old rule of composition. It says that the most visu-ally important places within any frame are located on the four lines that divide the frame in thirds.

When you compose a shot, begin by placing important visual elements on these lines. If you are shooting a landscape, frame the image so the horizon is on the top third or the lower third. See which you like. If you are shooting an interview, place the interviewee's eyes on the top third.

To really see how the rule of thirds is used, tape a piece of clear plastic over your television screen, and then use an erasable dry marker to draw four lines on it: two horizontal lines at the upper and lower third of the screen, and two vertical lines at the right and left third of the screen. Play any Hollywood movie, or watch any broadcast show and you will see immediately that *nearly every professional shot is composed on the rule of thirds.*

SECRET 13: **ADD PERSPECTIVE**

Whenever possible, look for ways to add perspective to your shots. Perspective gives your shots depth and interest. Look for something in the foreground that frames or somehow identifies the scene.

Common uses of perspective in films: train tracks that recede in the distance. Roads that recede in the distance. Lanes with trees or fence posts on the side of the road, in which the trees or fence posts recede in the distance.

SECRET 14: LOOK FOR DIAGONAL LINES

Another way to add visual interest to your shots is to look for compositional elements that add diagonal lines to your shots. The diagonal line will draw the viewer's eye, so you look for lines that lead the viewer's eye to the most important element in the picture.

SECRET 15: USE TRIANGLES

Painters have used triangles to give visual interest to paintings for hundreds of years. You can create a visual triangle by framing your shot so that three dominant elements in a scene are at the points of an imaginary triangle. The audience will subconsciously "create" a story from the three elements.

SECRET 16: CREATE LAYERED IMAGES

One of the most powerful techniques you can use to create compelling images is a "layered" image in which three elements are placed in spatial relationship to each other.

This technique is usually used with deep focus. In deep focus, everything in the scene is in sharp focus. Use a small f-stop to achieve deep focus. Deep focus is easy with most digital video cameras.

The front element in your image may be one character. Behind this character is a second character looking at the first character, and behind these two characters is a third character looking at the first two characters.

This technique is closely allied to the triangle technique. When you "layer" a scene, the audience will create relationships between the three layers and build a story in their mind. A layered image can be like a little visual gem, in which each facet reflects a different view of reality.

Layered images are an advanced technique to engage the viewer's imagination, and pull an audience slowly into a film.

CHAPTER 4

SUPPORTING AND MOVING THE CAMERA

How you support and move the camera is important.

Hand-held cameras, when used correctly, can give you marvelous footage that you can't get any other way. In the documentary War Tapes, director Deborah Scranton gave small Sony camcorders to three soldiers in a National Guard unit from New Hampshire just before their unit was deployed to Iraq. The resulting hand-held footage is powerful and emotionally moving. The technical quality of the images was good enough that the resulting digital footage (along with footage from a larger DV camera that Scranton used for interviews) was successfully transferred to 35mm film for the film's theatrical release.

Most of the time, however, hand-holding simply doesn't work. Shooting without a tripod often results in "jiggle cam" or even worse, "vomit cam."

This cliché was exploited to great effect in the pseudo-documentary *Blair Witch Project*. The movie was shot hand-held, and the camera jiggled and swerved, just like the shaky, hand-held shots of an amateur. The effect was so powerful that some teenagers who saw the movie thought that it was actual documentary footage.

In reality the movie was made by two extremely talented and skilled filmmakers who deliberately used this style to create believability.

If you remember only three words about camera movement, let them be these: use a tripod.

Placing the camera on a tripod and locking it down before each shot is a perfectly acceptable way to shoot your film.

SECRET 17: USE A TRIPOD

The standard advice for buying a tripod is "Get the best tripod you can afford."
Think of your tripod as an investment in your shooting career.

A good tripod will improve your shooting. It will be easier to set up, and you will be
able to level the camera quickly. Shots where you use the tripod will be rock-solid
and pans and tilts will be smooth and level.

Professional tripods have
a bubble on the "head"
(the part that holds
the camera) to tell you
when the tripod head is
level. The best tripods
have a "ball" mount so
you can quickly level
your camera. With a
ball mount, you don't
have to constantly
adjust the tripod legs to
level the camera. You
just set up the tripod
legs, loosen the ball and
swivel the tripod head to
level the camera. When
the camera is level,
simply re-tighten the
ball mount.

Heads are interchange-
able on high-end tripods.
Once you buy the "sticks" (tripod legs) you can buy new heads to accommodate different size cameras. Heads are usually rated by camera weight. The Miller Solo series,
for example, has heads designed for five-, ten- and twenty-pound cameras.

When you buy a tripod, buy one that is rated one step heavier than the camera you
plan to use. That gives you the latitude to upgrade to a larger camera or hang accessories, like heavy batteries and camera lights, on your existing camera.

Paradoxically, the lighter your camera, the heavier you want your tripod (within reason). When you attach a heavy tripod to the camera, the weight of the tripod helps steady the camera.

Many cameras also have OIS (Optical Image Stabilization) to help stabilize the camera. Modern OIS is amazing; it can smooth out "jiggly" hand-held images and give you brilliant footage. However, the best solution for rock-solid shooting—in most situations—is a good tripod.

When you mount the camera on a tripod, turn the camera's OIS "off." Otherwise, the OIS may "fight" the camera movement when you pan or tilt. This will show up as a slight "jump" in the image when the pan or tilt stops.

Filmmakers are vehement in their defense and preference for tripod brands. Try several at your local camera store, and find out which one appeals to you.

SECRET 18: USE A TILT

A "tilt" is a simple camera move, in which you move the camera slowly up or slowly down. In a tilt down, you start at the sky and slowly tilt down to reveal a character or scene. A tilt up starts at the ground and slowly moves up. The classic tilt-up starts with the shoe stepping out of a car, followed by a tilt up to reveal the leg of a gorgeous actress as she steps onto the sidewalk.

The key to doing a good tilt is to move the camera very slowly, much more slowly than you first imagine.

The best way to do a tilt is with a tripod, but you can do a tilt perfectly well using a hand-held camera.

Hold the camera in both hands and brace yourself against something like a wall. Take a deep breath and relax. Start recording and slowly tilt the camera.

SECRET 19: USE A PAN

A pan (sideways movement of the camera) is a way to follow a character as he or she walks through a scene.

The trick to doing a good pan is to move the camera slowly and give the character plenty of room in the frame as you move the camera. Don't allow the character to get too close to either edge of the frame as you are panning.

If you let the character get close to the leading edge of the frame, the image looks "crowded." If the character gets too close to the trailing edge of the frame the image looks "empty."

When you are shooting 24 frames per second, move the camera even slower. (Frame rates are described in Chapter 9, Choosing Camera Settings.) If you move the camera too fast when you are shooting 24 frames, the image will seem to "stutter" and "jump."

SECRET 20: SHOOT HAND-HELD

Hand-held footage is essential in many situations. If you are shooting a documentary, a wedding, or a guerilla no-budget independent film, you may not have the luxury of setting up a tripod for some shots.

The ability to shoot good hand-held footage is a learned skill. It does not come naturally. If you have a production coming up where you will need to shoot hand-held, take some time well before the shoot to learn how to get good hand-held footage.

With practice, you can get very smooth footage when shooting hand-held, especially if your camera has an Optical Image Stabilization (OIS) system. Image stabilization or a tripod is critical on a High Definition (HD) camera. The smallest amount of camera jiggle is visible to the audience in HD.

Here's an old cinematographer's trick that you can use to train yourself to walk smoothly. Practice walking around your house with a full bowl of water resting on your upturned palm. Try to walk everywhere without spilling the water. Walk forward, turn, crouch, stand up, and walk and up and down stairs. Keep at it until you can go everywhere without spilling the water. When you can do that, you will be able to shoot smooth hand-held footage.

Occasionally you might have to walk backwards while shooting hand-held. It can be very tricky to walk backwards while filming. Not only are you concentrating on the image, but you can't see where you are going!

When you absolutely have to walk backwards while filming, get a helper and ask him or her put a hand on your shoulder. Tell the helper be your eyes as you walk backwards. The helper's job will be to maintain physical contact and keep you from tripping, falling or running into things.

As you walk backwards, lift each foot straight up, move it back and then carefully step straight down. (It's easier than it sounds, especially with a helper's hand on your back.) Lifting your feet straight up reduces the chances of catching your heels on things and tripping.

SECRET 21: USE A DOLLY

A dolly (a wheeled cart) is a way to move in slowly on a scene. The word "dolly" refers both to the actual cart ("Let's get a dolly for that shot."), and to the act of moving in closer ("I'm going to dolly in.")

A dolly in can give your movie a wonderful feel of professionalism. Independent filmmakers have used many things for dollies: shopping carts, hand trucks, wheelchairs, and professional dollies rented from a movie equipment rental house.

Moving the camera closer to the subject generally gives you a better image than zooming. Moving closer looks natural, while zooming looks unnatural and tends to "flatten" perspective.

SECRET 22: USE A JIB

Another thing you can do to add visual interest to your movie quite cheaply is to use a jib (a long, weighted pole with the camera at one end.)

A jib is an easy way to have the camera start high above a scene and then float down, or start in the scene and then slowly rise above it.

With the advent of lightweight DV cameras, several manufacturers have introduced inexpensive, lightweight DV jibs.

CHAPTER 5

LIGHTING A SCENE FOR OPTIMAL EFFECT

Non-professionals need a system for analyzing lighting problems.

Available light
Secret 23: *Use the "big light in the sky" wisely*
Secret 24: *Bounce the light*
Secret 25: *Know what to do when available light is too low*
Secret 26: *Know what to do when available light is too high*

Artificial light
Secret 27: *Use three-point lighting*
Secret 28: *Learn how to use a basic lighting kit*
Secret 29: *Buy a quality lighting kit*
Secret 30: *Learn to use inexpensive artificial lights*
Secret 31: *Mix natural and artificial light*

COMMON LIGHTING PROBLEMS

Non-professional shooters can shoot badly lit shots for years because they don't have a system to analyze and correct lighting problems.

There are four things that often go wrong with video lighting.
- Too little light
- Too much light
- Lighting has the wrong ratio, direction or color
- White balance problems

Too little light

This is a very common problem. Modern cameras are so sensitive to light that we sometimes think they don't require any light, but they do. Inexpensive cameras, in particular, need a well-lighted scene to produce the best image.

Part of the "too little light" problem is our natural tendency to assume that the camera will record exactly what our eyes see. The eye sees much more than any video camera. When we try to record a dimly lit scene that our eye can see easily, the result is often a muddy, flat video image.

The best solution to "too little light" is to add light to the scene or to shoot in a different location.

If you can't do either of these things, you might decide to make the camera more sensitive to low light. You can try turning the video gain up, opening the camera aperture, and lowering the shutter speed. Each of these steps will change the look of the final image.

Another option to try is to recover an unexposed image in postproduction by using your video editing software to adjust contrast, brightness and color.

Too much light

When you have too much light, highlights and bright spots will be overexposed (blown out). An area that is blown out has no digital information within it and cannot be recovered in postproduction.

The only solution is to reduce the amount of light coming into the lens.

If you are shooting in available light you might move the subject into the shade, or wait until a different time of day, perhaps the twilight just around sunset.

Other ways you can reduce the amount of light entering the camera are adding neutral density (ND) filters, reducing the aperture, or increasing the shutter speed. (An ND filter reduces the amount of light without changing the color of the light.)

White balance problems

You know you have a white balance problem when your image is tinted the wrong color. The image may have an ugly blue, green, orange, yellow or golden tint.

The usual cure for this problem is to white balance your camera. (Chapter 9, Choosing Camera Settings, tells how to set white balance.)

Occasionally, you can correct a white balance problem in postproduction.

Lighting has the wrong ratio, direction or color

If the colors are right and you have enough light but the image is still not pleasing, you have a classic lighting problem.

The image may be brightly lit but flat, without shadows or modeling—the classic "evening news" lighting. Or the subject may be too harshly lit, with extreme shadows.

Pleasing lighting is about the amount, direction and color of the light that falls on a scene. Good lighting will create shadows that model the scene and give it visual interest and apparent depth.

The best contrast ratio for faces is about 4:1 (two f-stops difference between brightest and darkest areas of the image).

The classic lighting setup for creating this effect is three-point lighting. In three point lighting, the person is lighted from the back (back light), side (fill light), and front (key light) with three separate lights.

AVAILABLE LIGHT

Whenever possible, shoot with available light.

Available light simplifies the filmmaking process. Shoot several tests in available light, well before the shoot. Learn what works and what doesn't.

Shooting available light is not necessarily a shortcut. It may take more time than shooting with lights. You may spend a lot of time waiting for a certain time of day, or for certain weather to get just the light you need.

Here are a few films shot on available light.

Digital:
Full Frontal, Steven Soderbergh

Film:
All the Vermeers in New York, 1990, Jon Jost
El Mariachi, 1992, Robert Rodriguez
The Celebration, 1998, Thomas Vinterberg
Italian for Beginners, 2000, Lone Scherfig
Open Hearts, 2002, Susanne Bier

SECRET 23: USE THE "BIG LIGHT IN THE SKY" WISELY

When you shoot available light, one of your major light sources is the sun, the "big light in the sky." There are two problems with using the sun as your primary light.

The first problem is that the sun's light changes color as the sun moves through the sky. At sunrise, the sun gives a nice, soft, golden light. As noon approaches, the light gets "harder" and quite bluish. Toward sunset the light gets "softer" and golden again.

Filmmakers call the hours around sunrise and sunset the "golden hours." If you shoot in the golden hours, you can get a nice, soft light with a wonderful golden tone.

If you shoot during mid-day you will have a hard, bluish light.

When shooting outside in mid-day, look for a shaded area but avoid sun-dappled areas like those under a shade tree. The shaded areas will be properly exposed, but the sun-dappled spots will all be over-exposed.

When you shoot inside at mid-day, avoid south-facing windows (in the northern hemisphere). The mid-day light is so harsh that it can make people appear up to twenty years older.

The second problem is that the light coming from the sun changes direction as the sun moves.

This can be a problem when you shoot a long scene or interview. By the end of the interview the light is coming from a different direction. When you started shooting the light may have been falling on the interviewee's face, and by the end of the interview the light is coming over his shoulder.

This can cause problems when you edit the scene.

One way to compensate for the movement of the sun is to shoot on overcast days. On an overcast day the light is so diffuse that you won't notice the difference in light from one shot to the next.

SECRET 24: BOUNCE THE LIGHT

When you are shooting with available light, you often won't be able to get enough light on faces. The rule is, "If the eyes don't sparkle, you don't have enough light."

A simple way to get light up under the shelves of the eyebrows and make the eyes sparkle is to use a reflector to "bounce" some soft, gentle light back into the person's face.

Although you can use any white surface as a bounce reflector (white cardboard, or even a white three-ring binder), there are inexpensive commercial folding reflectors that you can carry with you when you go on your shoot. Some reflectors are two-sided: one side is silver and the other side is gold. The silver gives a harder, bluish light and the gold foil gives you a nice golden light.

SECRET 25: KNOW WHAT TO DO WHEN AVAILABLE LIGHT IS TOO LOW

When available light is too low, the digital video image will be noisy and the colors will begin to smear.

Ways to cope with low light:
- Add light. The first fix for low light is to get more light on the subject. Either add artificial light, or move to a location that has enough available light.
- Increase video gain. Turning up the camera's video gain increases the brightness of the image, and introduces video noise, which shows up as a grainy image. This is not always bad. Some filmmakers deliberately turn up the video gain because they like the grainy image. As a general rule, use video gain sparingly, and have a good reason. Otherwise it looks like cheap camera footage.
- Open the iris (increase the aperture by choosing a lower f-stop).
- Lower the shutter speed.

Different camcorders respond differently to low light. When you are choosing a camera, never go by the published low light numbers. Instead, shoot some tests in typical low light situations and see what the resulting image looks like.

SECRET 26: KNOW WHAT TO DO WHEN AVAILABLE LIGHT IS TOO HIGH

Excess light will over expose your image and "blow out" the highlights. Overexposed or "blown" areas in a video image are completely white, and contain no information. Blown areas cannot be fixed in postproduction.

There are four ways to deal with excess light.
- If your camera has zebra stripes, turn them on. Diagonal lines will appear in the viewfinder every place where the image is over-exposed. Close the iris—increase the f-stop—until the zebra stripes just barely disappear. (Zebra stripes are not recorded on the tape; they only show up in the viewfinder.)
- Use an ND (neutral density) filter to reduce the amount of light reaching the sensor. Many cameras have ND filters built in.
- Increase the shutter speed.

Using artificial light

The world won't cooperate when it comes to light. That's the simple truth.

Lighting, like sound, can be a lifetime affair. People study lighting for years to learn how to get it right. A book like *Matters of Light and Depth* by Ross Lowell is a good introduction to this discipline.

Meanwhile, here are a few basic things you can do.

SECRET 27: USE THREE-POINT LIGHTING

Three-point lighting is a basic, reliable method for lighting a simple scene. It uses three lights: a Key Light that highlights the key elements of the actor's face; the Fill Light that fills in the shadows on the actor's face; and the Back Light that lights the actor's back and separates him or her visually from the background.

SECRET 28: LEARN HOW TO USE A BASIC LIGHTING KIT

You can rent basic lighting kits quite cheaply. A basic lighting kit will include: key light, back light, fill light, stands (for holding the lights), and flags (metal shades to control where the light shines). It may also include a soft box (a specialized light that casts a wide, soft light) and reflectors.

SECRET 29: BUY A QUALITY LIGHTING KIT

If you choose to buy a lighting kit, buy a quality kit. A small kit with a soft boxes and umbrellas will give you about everything you need to light a simple interview or a small set.

Check out the Lowell DV Creator kits to see what a small kit should look like (at *http://www.lowel.com/kits/DVcreator1.html*).

These kits are not cheap, but if you do a lot of lighting, they are worth the money. You might also want to consider a custom hard case for the kit. A hard case is a good investment for hauling, organizing, and storing the lighting kit.

Whether you buy or rent a lighting kit, remember that lights can draw a lot of power. Before you shoot, check the fuses and breakers in the place where you will be filming. Make sure the electrical system can handle the additional load.

SECRET 30: LEARN TO USE INEXPENSIVE ARTIFICIAL LIGHTS

Some digital video filmmakers also use inexpensive light sources like:

- Chinese lanterns

- Work lamps from a hardware store
- Fluorescent lights (Careful! Flourescent lights may flicker)
- Flashlights
- LED camera lights that mount on the camcorder accessory shoe
- "Practicals." Practicals are large light bulbs that are color-corrected for video. They are used to replace tungsten bulbs in on-set lights like table lamps.

SECRET 31: MIX NATURAL AND ARTIFICIAL LIGHT

Occasionally, you will have to shoot in a place where you have both artificial and natural light. You may have sunlight coming through a window and light coming from a lamp on a table.

The best way to handle this is to white balance the camera in the mixed light. Place your white card next to the subject you will be filming, and press auto-white balance. After the camera is white balanced, turn white balance back to manual so it doesn't automatically re-balance.

Another way to handle this situation would be to place a "gel" over the window, changing the light coming through the window to "match" the tungsten lamp. A gel is a thin sheet of colored polycarbonate or polyester that is used to add a minor tint to light.

As a practical matter, you will probably only use three colors of gels, one each to match each the three white balance presets of your camcorder: tungsten, outside, and fluorescent.

The type of gel that you will be using is a "color correction" gel. You may see them referred to as CTB (Color Temperature Blue) and CTO (Color Temperature Orange.)

Two other gels you should know about are *ND* and *diffusion* gels.

ND gels reduce the amount of light falling on a scene, without changing its color. ND gels usually come in gray colored sheets. The higher the ND number, the darker the gray.

Diffusion gels soften the light falling on a scene, without changing its color. Diffusion gels usually come in translucent white sheets.

Manufacturers, like Roscoe, provide swatch kits of different gels.

CHAPTER 6

SHOOTING FOOTAGE THAT YOU CAN EDIT

You need more than pretty pictures when you shoot—you need shots that you can edit into a compelling movie.

Goats are intelligent, friendly animals. As a large goat walked past she turned her head and looked at me curiously. I quickly added a note to my shot list, "goat investigates." (A "shot list" is just a list of all the shots you plan to shoot in a certain location or scene.)

I was visiting a small goat dairy in Northern California to scout the location and make a shot list for a documentary. It was a beautiful spring day. Sleek dairy goats grazed in green fields, and the hillsides were covered with wildflowers.

The cameraman was a little nervous about the upcoming shoot. He had never been on a goat dairy in his life. Two days later, on the morning of the shoot, I gave him the shot list. Then we walked through the dairy and reviewed the shots.

When he was satisfied, he got his camera and set up for the day's shooting.

Our first shot was of the farmer leading a herd of goats to the milking barn. Suddenly, the large goat spotted the cameraman. She left the herd and ambled over to the cameraman. The cameraman freaked out, but kept the camera running. We got a great shot of "goat investigates" as the goat sniffed the lens.

We left the dairy with two pounds of gourmet cheese and an hour of excellent footage. We were able to get everything we needed in one day's shooting: close-ups, medium shots, establishing shots and cutaways.

SECRET 32: MAKE A SHOT LIST BEFORE YOU SHOOT

The apparently simple act of making a shot list draws upon all the elements of good filmmaking:

1. Knowing your subject intimately
2. Knowing what story you are telling
3. Visualizing your movie.

Knowing your subject intimately may take a considerable amount of research. You may not be able to make a good shot list until after you have done an Internet search, interviewed several people, read a few books and magazines, and spent some time in the field or on location.

After you've done your research, the next step is to visualize the story and "see" the movie in your mind, from start to finish. Your visualization should show you the long shots, medium shots and close-ups.

You may want to create a storyboard to record your vision. The storyboard does not have to be very polished; a rough sketch will do. A rough storyboard is a way to quickly reveal all the shots you need to tell your story.

Sometimes you shoot without a shot list

Rarely, you just start shooting, without a shot list. Your shooting is part of your research.

You begin by writing a brief list of subjects you'd like to shoot, and then simply take your camera and go out and shoot some footage.

Afterwards, watch the footage on your computer. You will like some, hate some, and most will leave you neutral.

Assemble the bits you like into a little movie.

Repeat the process of shooting, reviewing and assembling until you see a story emerging from the footage.

This process can lead to powerful footage and unexpected insights. It can also lead to a unique way of "seeing" the world, because you are filming without pre-conceptions.

This method is a good way to get things moving and break out of "paralysis by analysis." The big danger in this process is that you may waste a lot of time before you find your story.

SECRET 33: GET THE ESSENTIAL IMAGES

Before you shoot, go through your shot list and identify the "must-have" shots. You might want to plan a way to get these shots, no matter what else happens.

Shots to consider:
- Establishing shot of the location
- Master shot of the activity or scene (a wide shot that shows the entire scene)
- Medium shots of the essential activities
- Close-ups of essential people
- Close-ups of essential details
- "Once in a lifetime" shots (the bride and groom's first kiss, a marathon runner crossing the finish line, the only interview with a celebrity or key person)

SECRET 34: SHOOT SEQUENCES

Everything happens in sequences—whether it's cooking a meal, driving a car, or meeting someone for lunch. Always look for the sequences in what you shoot. Try to get each activity from beginning to end.

When we were on the goat dairy, we shot the entire goat-milking sequence from the time the goats left the pen to the time the milk swirled into a stainless steel vat. Then we filmed the sequence by which the milk was turned into wheels of cheese.

You may not use all the shots in a sequence when you edit your film, but you will have them if you need them. Invariably, you never know which ones you will need until it's too late to re-shoot.

SECRET 35: GET REACTION SHOTS

Reaction shots are close-ups of people's emotional reactions.

Any candid, spontaneous expression of emotion may give you a powerful image that will affect an audience deeply.

When shooting an independent film, some directors shoot scenes twice to get the reaction shots. The first time through the camera focuses on one actor's face. The second time through the camera is focuses on another actor's face. In postproduction, the two shots are edited together to make a seamless story.

When you are shooting an event or a wedding, try to get a few close-ups of people's reactions as events unfold. Adding candid reaction shots into your footage often gives the final video increased emotional power and intimacy.

SECRET 36: **SHOOT MOTIVATED CUTAWAYS**

A cutaway is a picture of something in the environment that you can "cut" to when editing a scene.

Cutaways work best when they are "motivated," and have a reason to be in the film.

For example, an interviewee may become very nervous during an interview and start twisting his or her watch around her wrist.

A close-up of the interviewee's hands as he or she twists the watch would be a motivated cutaway, because it gives a hint of the interviewee's mental state.

Oddly enough, cutaways to animals, like a cat turning to look at the camera, or a dog panting, almost always work.

SECRET 37: **MAINTAIN A LOW SHOOTING RATIO**

Your "shooting ratio" is the amount of footage you shoot compared to the amount of footage in your final film. If you shoot twenty minutes of video to make a one-minute film, your shooting ratio is 20:1.

The lowest possible shooting ratio is 1:1. Your final film is what you shoot. All editing is done "in camera."

The skill of shooting "in camera" (planning all your shots, and shooting them one after the other) is a useful skill to have. It is a way to shoot a movie quickly and cheaply, but it's difficult and demands good visualization skills.

Sometimes you can't keep a low shooting ratio. When you are shooting a documentary, you may not have any choice except to shoot *lots* of footage in hopes of getting the few moments that you need to tell your story.

The higher the shooting ratio, the longer it is going to take you to finish your film. For one thing, someone has to log all the footage and make decisions on how to use it.

SECRET 38: LABEL YOUR MEDIA

Label everything as you go!

Label your tapes and other media with:
1. Date
2. Name of shot or scene
3. Your name
4. Your phone number

The ideal is to have labels that are clear enough that you could put your script or treatment and all your tapes a box, hand the box to an editor and walk away. The editor should have enough information from the labels and the treatment or script to make a good first cut of the film.

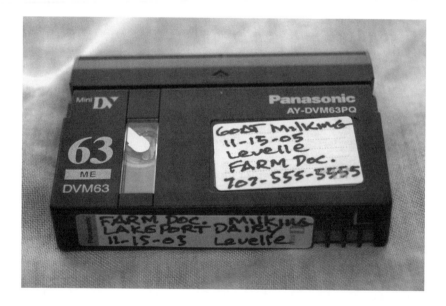

SECRET 39: SLATE YOUR SHOTS

Slating is the practice of taking a five-second picture of a white board or slate at the beginning of each shot.

The slate can be as simple as a piece of white paper that lists the subject of the shot, the date and other essential information. With slates at the head of each shot, you can easily identify shots and scenes when you sit down to edit.

Without a slate, you may spend hours figuring out when a particular shot was taken, and why it was made.

The slate should include:

1. Date
2. Time
3. Name of shot or scene
4. Notes (optional)
5. "Take" number (if you are doing multiple takes.)
6. Your name

CHAPTER 7

GETTING GOOD SOUND

Sound is important, really important.

Location sound

Secret 40: The smaller your crew, the more you need a dedicated sound person

Secret 41: Consider hiring a professional sound person

Secret 42: Scout all locations for sound

Secret 43: Know how to use the on-camera mike

Secret 44: Use a professional field recorder

Secret 45: Use good headphones

Directional microphones

Secret 46: Consider using boomed directional mikes for dialog

Secret 47: Use a boom

Secret 48: Shotgun microphone on a camera

Secret 49: Always use wind screens on your microphones

Lavaliere microphones

Secret 50: Consider lavaliere mikes for dialog

Secret 51: Where to put the lavaliere microphone

Secret 52: Wired lavaliere microphones

Secret 53: Wireless lavaliere microphones

Filmmakers tend to think visually. This is a powerful asset when it comes to visualizing a film, scene or shot, but it can be an equally powerful handicap when it comes to sound. Because we can't see sound, we tend to ignore it: Out of sight, out of mind.

The audience, however, responds to a film differently. The audience responds first to the *sound*.

New filmmakers almost always underestimate the importance and difficulty of getting good sound.

They may say, "We'll fix the sound problems in post," but fixing sound in post (post production) often doesn't work.

For one thing, your actors or talent are emotionally involved at the moment you are shooting. That involvement may be difficult or impossible to recreate in a recording studio weeks or months after the original shoot.

If the original sound is too low, and the dialog is "in the mud," raising sound levels in post will only amplify all the background noise without improving the dialog.

Noise or reverberation (echoes) on a sound track may be impossible to fix in post. The most common fixes for noise and reverberation have to be done on location. They include things like eliminating the noise source, using different microphones, hanging heavy blankets on the walls or shooting in a different location.

Fortunately, decent sound is possible, even on a budget. The trick is to decide, from the beginning, that sound is as important as the images.

Location sound is important

On a documentary, location sound is everything. You may add narration or sound effects later, but the dialog and interviews you capture on location are irreplaceable.

Location sound is just as important to a low-budget, small-crew feature film. What you get on location is often what you may end up using for the film's sound track.

ADR (automated dialog replacement in a studio) happens all the time in Hollywood. With trained actors and a full recording studio, it's a great way to get stunning dialog. However, ADR is an expensive, labor-intensive process, and is not a realistic option for most small-crew independent films.

Let's look at some of the things you can do to improve your chances of getting good sound.

SECRET 40: THE SMALLER YOUR CREW, THE MORE YOU NEED A DEDICATED SOUND PERSON

The smaller your crew, the more you need a dedicated sound person. (Everyone resists this, including me, but I still believe it is true.) Here's why:

- Sound is one of the two most likely things that will mess you up. (The other is story.)
- Good sound will increase your movie's production values like nothing else.
- Good sound takes less postproduction time. (It takes *forever* to fix sound problems, and many are unfixable.)
- Sound recording is at least as difficult as cinematography. A good sound person will spend years mastering the craft.
- A dedicated sound person may be cheap when you compare the cost to the total expense of your film or production.
- No one on the set except the sound person will be looking at the sound.
- A good sound person will be able to hear things in the sound—good and bad—that no one else on the set will notice.

SECRET 41: CONSIDER HIRING A PROFESSIONAL SOUND PERSON

Even if you can't afford to hire a professional for your whole film, it may be worthwhile to hire a professional as a consultant.

Go over your plans for the shoot. Ask for advice on the types of microphones you should use, where to place them and how exactly to record the microphone's output.

Things to look for in a sound professional:
- Experience working on films or productions like yours
- A good portfolio of sound tracks
- A willingness to work on independent, low-budget productions
- A desire to work on *your* production

SECRET 42: SCOUT ALL LOCATIONS FOR SOUND

When you scout your shooting locations, scout for sound, too. Many noise problems happen at a particular time of day, like a club that plays loud music from
10PM to 2AM, or jet planes that only land at a certain time of day. Try to scout the
location at the same time of day that you plan to shoot.

The two main problems with location sound are noise and reverberation. Take a
camcorder or a field recorder with you and record a few minutes of sound in the
exact spots where you intend to shoot. Play the recording back later and listen for
potential problems.

First, listen for noise. Noise can come from anywhere. Refrigerators. Air condition-
ers. Airplanes. Buses in the street. Traffic from nearby freeways. Floors creaking.
Dogs barking.

If the location is noisy, the first option is to eliminate the noise sources. This may
be as simple as turning off an air conditioner or a refrigerator during an interview. When you can't eliminate the noise source you should probably think about
moving to another location.

If the location has reverberation (echoes), see if hanging heavy blankets on the
walls will fix the problem. If you can't get rid of the reverberation, look for another
location.

SECRET 43: KNOW HOW TO USE THE ON-CAMERA MIKE

The on-camera microphone on your camcorder is of limited use. If you have a
choice, do not use it for recording dialog. You can use it for dialog in a very limited
set of circumstances, described below.

The things the on-camera microphone is good for include:
- Ambient (background) sounds
- "Scratch tracks" (a low-quality dialog track, used as a reference during
  sound and picture editing)
- Production effects (A recording of the overall sounds in a location. For
  example, as you shoot a wide shot of a truck stop, the camera captures the
  sounds of trucks pulling off the highway and driving past. This recording
  might be mixed into your final track as background sound.)

- In an emergency, you can use the on-camera microphone for interviews. Here's how:

  Do the interview in a quiet place.

  Open the lens wide.

  Get the camera as close to the person as possible. If you can get the camera very close and still get a good picture, you might get acceptable sound.

Unless you have no other option, *do not* use the microphone on the camcorder as your primary microphone for dialog. The placement of the microphone is wrong (too far from the person speaking), and most camera microphones do not have the quality you need for an outstanding sound track.

SECRET 44: USE A PROFESSIONAL FIELD RECORDER

If you decide to record your sound on a separate recorder, it might be worth your while to look at buying a low-end professional audio field recorder like those made by Tascam or Roland. Prices begin around $1,100 and go up from there.

A professional audio recorder will have the following features:
- Excellent sound quality
- Easy to use, intuitive user interface
- Volume meters for each channel
- XLR jacks for professional microphone connections
- Accurate, rock-solid recording times
- Time code inputs. (A few high-end prosumer cameras generate a time code that a field recorder uses to synchronize the audio to the camera's time code. The recorder's sound track and the camera's image track are always in exact alignment.)
- Removable flash memory cards
- Durable and rugged, will survive rough treatment on location

Avoid using consumer audio recorders and inexpensive MP3 player/recorders for filmmaking. Their audio track is not time-coded and are difficult to synchronize with the images being recorded by the camera. An inexpensive recorder may be off as much as one or two seconds an hour. Instead of recording a full sixty minutes, the actual recording may be plus or minus a second. This doesn't sound like much, but it's enough to drive you crazy when you are editing the show, and suddenly realize you have lost *lip-sync,* and the actors' lips are moving slightly before or after you hear the dialog.

If you have to use a consumer recorder for sound, make sure you slate the sound at the beginning of each shot. To slate the sound, use a clapper slate. When you edit the show, you can synchronize the sound by aligning the sound of the clapper closing with the image of the clapper closing.

I use a toy clapper slate that I found in a movie poster store.

SECRET 45: **USE GOOD HEADPHONES**

When you are in the field, someone should listen to all the sound as it is recorded. If you are running a "one man band," this person will be you. If you are lucky enough to have a dedicated sound person, that person will be listening to all the sound.

The best way to listen is with a good pair of studio headphones. Studio headphones make it easier to focus only on the sound because they cover your ears completely.

When you first listen to location sound with headphones, you might hear a large amount of background noise and hiss in the signal. Background noise and hiss tends to sound louder in headphones because the source of the sound is close to your eardrums. When you play the same sound back on normal speakers, you may not be able to hear the noise. This phenomenon is so common that it even has a name, "the headphone effect."

if you think you have "headphone effect," record some sound and play it back on a good audio system. If you don't hear the hiss when the sound comes over the speakers, you probably had headphone effect.

Directional microphones

SECRET 46: CONSIDER USING BOOMED DIRECTIONAL MIKES FOR DIALOG

Directional (shotgun) microphones are the long, directional (picks up sound primarily from one direction) microphones that you sometimes see hanging from a long "boom" (pole) that extends over the actor or talent.

A directional microphone will pick up good dialog from up to a couple feet away. The pickup patterns of directional microphones vary. Experiment with different microphones until you find the one with a sound that appeals to you.

SECRET 47: USE A BOOM

A good way to use a shotgun microphone is to attach it to a boom and have some-one "boom" the microphone. The preferred way to boom the microphone is to hold the microphone over the speaker, with the microphone pointing down at the speaker.

The boom operator should keep the microphone as close as possible to the speaker, without allowing the microphone to appear in the picture.

The job of boom operator is much more difficult than it appears. It requires physical strength and sensitivity to what is being filmed.

When the camera pulls back for a wider shot, the boom operator has to move the microphone up to keep it out of the picture. When the camera moves in, the boom operator has to move the microphone in closer at the same time.

SECRET 48: PUT A SHOTGUN MICROPHONE ON THE CAMERA

Another option for a directional (shotgun) microphone is to mount it on the camera. Some cameras come with special mounts just for this arrangement. The microphone is usually held above the camera in a rubberized holder that protects the microphone from camera noise.

This arrangement gives okay sound in some situations. The microphone still has to be fairly close to the interviewee, or the sound will be muffled.

SECRET 49: ALWAYS USE WIND SCREENS ON YOUR MICROPHONES

The slightest breeze or movement of air can cause wind noise as the air moves over the microphone. It's not just a problem with recording outside. Air movement within a room can also cause wind noise.

You should assume that you need a wind screen all the time.

The directional microphone in this picture is covered with a nice soft Rycote Softie wind screen.

Lavaliere microphones

Lavaliere microphones are tiny microphones that are usually clipped to the actor or talent's clothing, or taped to their bodies. They are usually placed between six and nine inches from the chin of the person speaking, but not within the audio shadow of the chin. Many reality shows use wireless lavaliere microphones.

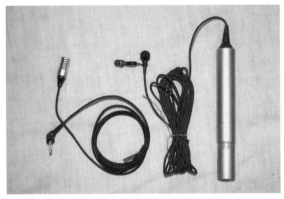

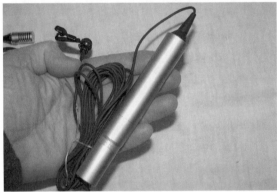

SECRET 50: CONSIDER LAVALIERE MIKES FOR DIALOG

Lavaliere mikes are often your best, most useful solution for recording dialog. The lavaliere microphone can be taped underneath clothing if you don't want it to show on camera. Use bandages to tape the microphone to the skin.

A large problem with lavaliere microphones is clothing noise. When the actor or interviewee moves, clothing rubs on the microphone. One way to prevent this is to tape the clothing in place with double-stick surgical tape to hold it in one place.

Another problem with a lavaliere microphone is when the subject turns his head to the side while speaking. As the head turns, the volume falls off. Normally, this is corrected in post. One way to cope with this problem is to use a directional microphone in addition to the lavaliere microphone.

Record the signal from the directional microphone to a separate track. That way, if the lavaliere signal is distorted by clothing noise or if the volume falls off, you can use the sound from the directional microphone.

SECRET 51: WHERE TO PUT THE LAVALIERE MICROPHONE

When you wire someone with a lavaliere microphone, you generally want the microphone six to nine inches from the person's mouth, but not in the audio shadow of the jaw. Put the microphone as close to the center line of the person's body as possible.

If the person is sitting sideways to the camera, and will be looking at the camera while speaking, tape the microphone on the side toward the camera.

SECRET 52: WIRED LAVALIERE MICROPHONES

A wired microphone is one that is connected to your camcorder or audio recorder by a wire. Wired mikes are simple, inexpensive and don't have any issues with transmission, interference, or signal reflection.

The disadvantage of wired microphones is that the actor or interviewee is tethered to the recorder (or camcorder) by a cable.

People tend to freeze up and move stiffly when they are wired because they fear they might break something if they move suddenly.

Some wired microphones come with a preamplifier that boosts the signal coming from the microphone before it is sent to the recorder.

Preamplifiers usually run on AA or AAA batteries.

It's a good idea to put a new battery in the preamplifier before each interview or recording session, and to bring a couple new batteries with you as spares, just in case.

SECRET 53: WIRELESS LAVALIERE MICROPHONES

Wireless microphones are more complicated and expensive than wired microphones, but they are very convenient.

You just clip the transmitter on someone's belt, plug the microphone into the transmitter, and a matching receiver on the camcorder feeds the audio directly to the camcorder's audio input.

With a wireless microphone people can move about freely without worrying about getting tangled in audio cables.

A wireless microphone is also a good way to get a microphone into places where there is simply no way you could use a wired microphone.

The disadvantages of wireless microphones are several:
- Cost. You not only have to pay for a good microphone, you have to pay for a transmitter and receiver of equal quality.
- Complexity. You have more things to go wrong: Transmitter, receiver, cables, and connectors.
- Radio Frequency Interference (RFI) from other wireless sources and some electronic devices.
- Transmission path problems. Occasionally, the camera-mounted receiver won't pick up a good signal from the transmitter. One solution is to move the receiver away from the camera and run a cable from the receiver to the camera.

CHAPTER 8

USING TEST CHARTS AND CARDS

Test cards and charts are not just for professionals.

Secret 54: Use a spectroscopically neutral white card

Secret 55: Learn to use a warming white card

Secret 56: Use a colorbar and grayscale chart

Secret 57: Use a focus chart

Secret 58: Learn to use your waveform monitor

Test cards and charts are not just for professionals

> "Shell out a few bucks and buy yourself a chart. It will serve you well for years to come and go further toward helping you develop and define a consistent 'look' than any other single investment."
>
> Scott Billups, *Digital Moviemaking* (2nd Edition)

Along with all the "professional" features packed into inexpensive HD cameras come some professional problems: getting consistently accurate color, focus, white balance, and a high-quality video signal.

The pros use three tools to get high quality video: a *grayscale/colorbar chart*, a *focus chart* and a *white balance card*.

How do you know if you need a chart? You might need a chart if:

- You need a color reference at the beginning of each shot because you are shooting a feature film or documentary and plan to color balance the final film.
- You want to get the best picture possible.
- You plan to spend lot of time in postproduction.
- You are a technically inclined enthusiast who wants a way to look at your video signal and tweak it for maximum effect.
- You are a video artist and you need an objective way to look at the video signal and manipulate it.

SECRET 54: USE A SPECTROSCOPICALLY NEUTRAL WHITE CARD

If you can only own one chart or card, get a true white card like the DSC Labs CamWhite card (*www.dsclabs.com*).

Manually white balance every shot in the same light that you will be shooting. If the light changes, re-balance the camera.

When you manually white balance your camera to a pure white card, you align the camera's colorimetric (color reproducing circuits) to do the best job possible in reproducing the color in the scene.

You should always use a commercial white balance card to manually white balance your camera. Something that just "looks" white—a T-shirt, sheet of copier paper or the back of a business card—may subtly distort the way a camera reproduces colors.

What appears white to our eyes usually has a slight color tint. When you use a tinted surface for white balancing, the camera's white reference point is off, and the resulting image coming out of the camera will be slightly tinted. It may have an overall bluish, greenish, or yellowish tint.

When you white balance with a pure white card, skin tones are reproduced with accuracy, and your camera's color reproduction is optimized. A signal with optimal color saves time in postproduction.

SECRET 55: LEARN TO USE A WARMING WHITE CARD

When you white balance with a card that has a slight bluish tint, the camera's colorimetric circuits are "fooled" into producing a warmer image with more attractive skin tones. This warmer image helps avoid the common television problem of cold, unattractive skin tones.

The DSC Labs *White and Warm Chart* has the precise tint needed to get pleasing skin tones.

SECRET 56: USE A COLORBAR AND GRAYSCALE CHART

A colorbar and grayscale chart like the DSC CamAlign FrontBox chart is a tool to
help you to reproduce the colors of a scene accurately.

To use the chart, place it in the same lighting that you will be shooting under. Zoom
in until the chart fills the viewfinder. Record a second or two of the chart.

Several prosumer editing programs (Final Cut Pro and others) have vectorscopes.

When you edit the footage, open the vectorscope function and look at the signal
generated by the FrontBox image.

With the FrontBox signal as a reference you can use a vectorscope to make accurate and repeatable color adjustments in postproduction.

SECRET 57: USE A FOCUS CHART

HD is notoriously unforgiving about focus. Any misfocus will show up immediately
on a high definition screen. A focus chart is one way to set focus exactly. (See
Chapter 9, Choosing Camera Settings, for more ways to set focus.)

There are many different types of focus patterns, but a basic pattern that seems to
work well is the star chart.

If you decide to buy a DSC CamAlign Front Box chart, get a star chart on the reverse side and you'll have both of the charts that you need.

To use the star chart, place it next to your talent or subject. Zoom in. and adjust focus until the star "pops" into focus in the viewfinder. Either adjust the focus manually, or press the "auto focus once" button and let the camera do the focusing for you.

SECRET 58: LEARN TO USE YOUR WAVEFORM MONITOR

Several high-end consumer editing programs include waveform monitors and vector-scopes. These tools are the fastest, most reliable way to analyze a video signal.

The editing program will come with detailed instructions on how to use the wave-form monitor, so I'll just talk about the waveform monitor, vectorscope and audio monitor in general—what they are, what they do, and why you might want to learn to use them.

Don't worry too much about the technical terms. The best way to learn about vector-scopes and waveform monitors is to open the editing program and play with them.

Waveform monitors are used to display and measure the overall video signal. Modern waveform monitors consist of three main elements: waveform monitor, vectorscope, and audio signal monitor.

The waveform monitor is also used to analyze the signal to make sure that it meets certain technical standards for broadcast.

The vectorscope is used to visualize the video signal's chrominance. Chrominance is the part of the video signal that carries the color information. The signal is displayed on a circular display. Six boxes on the circular display represent the six colors on the color chart. The six colors are indicated by six dots. When the colors are adjusted properly, the dots are in the exact center of the boxes.

Aligning the signal from different shots, scenes, or cameras is a matter of moving the dots into the boxes. When the dots from different video signals are each within the boxes, the colors in the two different signals will look alike.

The audio monitor measures the difference between the channels of a stereo audio signal. One channel drives the horizontal display of the monitor, and the other channel drives the vertical display of the channel.

CHAPTER 9

CHOOSING CAMERA SETTINGS

The only three settings you really have to understand, and a really, really brief introduction to the rest of the settings.

This chapter talks about the most important manual controls, and briefly describes the more advanced controls.

Most of us will never have the time to learn how to use all the advanced controls on a top-end prosumer camera. Fortunately, in most situations you only need to know how to use a few of the advanced controls.

And, if you really have to, you can just shoot full auto!

SECRET 59: LEARN HOW TO USE FULL AUTO

Let me start this discussion with a flat statement: manual settings are the only way to get consistently good images. But sometimes you have no choice but full auto mode.

You may have to shoot immediately, with no time to adjust the camera's settings. It may be something that is only going to happen once, like the baby's first step.

Full auto is even used by choice in some documentary footage, when the filmmaker may not want to draw attention to him or herself or the camera. Usually, the only way a filmmaker can get away with shooting full auto is if the subject is so compelling that the audience does not notice the bad footage.

How to shoot "full auto"

1. Turn the camera on and press the "Easy" or "Auto" button. (Different cameras have different buttons for this function.)
2. Start recording.
3. Hold the camera as steady as possible, and keep the subject in the center of the frame.
4. Try to maintain a steady distance from the subject while you are recording.
5. Use an external microphone. When you can't use an external microphone, get the camera as close as practical to the source of the sound.
6. Fingers off the zoom while recording.
7. Keep the dominant source of light behind you or to one side. Don't shoot strongly backlit subjects.
8. When shooting dark skin tones in auto mode consider using the AE shift option (if your camera has it) to bump the exposure up an f-stop or two.

Common auto mode problems

The camera pans (moves) across a room and the footage is fine until the pan reaches a window. Suddenly, everything else in the room goes dark as the camera adjusts its exposure to the flood of light pouring though the window.

The image goes in and out of focus as the camera "hunts" for focus.

The image has a weird yellowish, bluish, greenish, or orange tint. This is usually a sign of a white balance problem.

The image is dark and noisy. There isn't enough light for a decent image, and the camera is cranking up the video gain.

The sound has strong hiss during quiet parts. The AGC is cranking the audio gain up when things get quiet.

Manual mode—basic settings

The only way to get consistently good footage is by learning to set the manual settings.

Fortunately, there are only three manual settings you really need to know: focus, aperture, and white balance.

If you set these three things properly, you will get excellent footage 80% of the time.

The easy way to shoot all manual

Note: You won't break anything by changing any of these settings.

1. White balance the camera using a commercial white card. As soon as the camera is white balanced, turn auto white balance OFF. If the light changes, re-balance.
2. Zoom in on the part of the scene you want to be in focus. Turn on auto focus. When the camera finds focus, switch back to manual focus.
3. Zoom out and reframe.
4. Turn on auto exposure. The camera will set what it thinks is the ideal exposure. Switch auto exposure OFF. Adjust the aperture up or down a couple clicks to fine-tune the exposure to your liking.

SECRET 60: LET THE CAMERA TELL YOU THE EXPOSURE

When you set exposure you have three choices: expose for highlights at the expense of shadows, expose for shadows at the expense of highlights, or let the camera choose an automatic setting that gives you an average the whole scene.

Generally, people expose to "preserve the highlights" because viewers will notice "blown" (all white) highlights in an image before they notice shadows without detail.

To use the camera to set exposure:
1. Zoom in on the most important part of the scene.
2. Turn on auto exposure and let the camera find the ideal aperture (f-stop).
3. Switch back to manual exposure.
4. Zoom back out and reframe.
5. Tweak the exposure a couple clicks up or down.
   — If you want to show more detail in the shadows, open up the aperture one step at a time.
   — If you want more detail in the highlights, close down the aperture one step at a time.

Exposure tips

Given that there are no cut and dried recipes for "perfect exposure" here are a few tips and tricks:
- Exposing properly is an art. You get better at it as you practice, develop your eye and get a feel for your camera.
- Other things you can do to get better at exposure are to study well-exposed video and film and read photography books. In your reading, make sure that you read the Ansel Adams books on the Zone System.
- If your camera has zebra stripes, turn them on. Set your zebra stripes at 100. Close the iris gradually until zebra stripes just begin to appear on the highlights in the image. From this point you have three choices:
  1. Leave it that way to get a well-exposed picture with good contrast and a few areas that are "blown."
  2. Turn the iris back down until no zebras appear, to get a picture which may be a little less contrasty with no "blown" areas.
  3. Open the iris *more* to get a picture with many "blown" areas and relatively higher contrast in the remaining "unblown" areas.

You will get three distinct "looks" this way. None of them is "better" than the other, and each is a distinct creative choice.

- HDV does not have a lot of latitude for wide variations for light, so you have to be very careful when you set exposure.
- The LCDs on most consumer cameras are way too bright when they come from the factory. You should fix this by turning down the LCD brightness. Connect your camera to a good monitor or television and adjust the brightness of the LCD until the image in the LCD is closer to what you see on the big screen.
- When you shoot outside, you are always fighting a battle with lighting. The dynamic range of a brightly lit day is so wide that you often have to choose between exposing the sky, the ground, the foreground, or the background. One way to overcome the brightness of the sky is a graduated ND filter (it reduces the light in the top half of the image without affecting color). This way you preserve the detail in the sky.
- Prosumer and consumer cameras work best in properly lit settings. They generally don't do well in poorly lit situations. As long as you are working with inexpensive cameras you will always have to compromise on exposure. Just do the best you can.
- If you are shooting in bright light (usually outside), use the camera's built-in ND (Neutral Density) filters inside the lens to reduce the amount of light reaching the camera's image sensor. An ND filter reduces the amount of light, without changing the light's color in any way.

SECRET 61: DON'T WORRY ABOUT SHUTTER SPEED

Most of the time you really don't need to worry about the camera's shutter speed. The only time you need to adjust the shutter speed is when you are looking for a specific effect.

Unless you select a shutter speed manually, the shutter speed will default to the "standard" speed for the frame rate that you are shooting. (NTSC, PAL, and film-look frame rates are defined in Secret 66.) The standard speeds are:
1/60 for an NTSC camera
1/50 for a PAL camera
1/48 for a camera shooting 24 frames (film-look).

Shutter speed tips

- Higher shutter speeds can be very useful if you want to shoot scenes with rapid movement—like sports or car races on bright days. Generally, in this situation the more light you have and the faster your shutter speed, the sharper and clearer your picture will be.
- If you set the shutter speed very high (say around 1/1000), you get jerky movement, like the effect in *Saving Private Ryan*.
- If you set the shutter speed very low (say around 1/4 or 1/2 second), you get blurred movement. Some filmmakers like this effect and use it to create impressionistic shots where any movement becomes a swirling stream of color.
- If you are shooting in very low light, try dividing the standard shutter speed by half as a way to get more light to the sensor. Try 1/30 for NTSC, 1/25 for PAL, or 1/24 for 24 frame.

SECRET 62: SET WHITE BALANCE MANUALLY

Your camera has no way of knowing what "pure white" is unless you tell it. Once you tell the camera what "pure white" is in a certain situation, it uses that setting as a reference point to generate the colors in the video image.

White balance is a normal user setting, so do not be afraid to use it. You can't break anything.

The fast easy way to white balance manually

1. Take off all filters except your UV filter.
2. Place your white chart in the same light under which you will be filming.
3. Zoom in and fill the screen with the white chart.
4. Turn on auto white balance and let the camera set the white balance.
5. Switch back to manual white balance.
6. Zoom out and reframe.
7. White balance every time the light changes (this could mean before each shot.)

White balance tips

- Most camcorders have three preset white balance settings: Exterior, Tungsten, and Fluorescent. If you can't manually white balance before each shot, use one of these three presets for all your shots. The colors won't be as accurate as if you manually white balanced before each shot, but they will be consistent. You can fine-tune any color differences in post.

- On rainy days, the "Exterior" white balance preset may not be very accurate. On rainy, overcast days it's a good idea to manually white balance with a chart like the DSC Labs White'nWarm (*www.dsclabs.com*).

- Sunrise and sunset. Try auto white balance when shooting during the "golden hours" of sunrise and sunset. If you manually white balance during these hours, you may lose the "golden" tones.

- Some people white balance with an off-white white card to fool the white balance. Light blue gives an image with warmer tones, and light yellow gives an image with cooler tones.

- If you plan to have your video transferred to film, don't use an off-white card to "fool" the white balance. Instead, always use a neutral white card when you white balance.

- Always read your camera's instruction manual for an explanation of white balance, and how it is set.

SECRET 63: DOUBLE CHECK YOUR FOCUS

Focus is critical when shooting HD. An interlaced 1080-line (1080i) image contains enough information to fill a fifty-inch flat screen with a richly detailed image. At this level of detail, out-of-focus shots are glaringly obvious.

If the only tool you have to tell whether you are in focus is the LCD, you are in trouble. The LCD is so small that you can't really tell whether the image is really in focus. The only real option you have—other than having a large high-definition monitor on site—is using the camera's auto focusing circuits to set focus.

Focusing with the "push to focus" button
Push-to focus is a feature on many cameras that allows you to engage auto focus momentarily.

To use push-to-focus:
- Zoom in on the area you want to be in focus.
- Press the push-to-focus button. (Some cameras require holding the button for a couple seconds.)
- Switch to manual focus.
- Zoom out and reframe.

Focusing with focus assist

Most HD cameras have a focus assist feature that you can use to set accurate focus. Each camera implements focus assist differently.

- Enlargement electronically enlarges the central area of the image as you adjust the focus.
- Edge enhancement outlines any edges in the central part of the image in contrasting colors. As you turn the focus ring, the colors change to show you when you are in focus.
- Touch-screen focusing is a fairly new method. If your camera has touch screen focusing, you touch a spot on the LCD to tell the camera where to focus, and the camera focuses on that spot automatically.

Manual mode—advanced settings

Many of the cameras that allow you to change advanced settings also have a way to record and store your changes. That way you only have to do the manual settings once, and you can re-use them as needed.

Some cameras store the changes internally as "scene settings," while other cameras store the settings on removable flash memory, like an SD card.

With the settings stored on an SD card, you can quickly transfer the settings to other cameras of the same model, or save the settings for future shoots.

SECRET 64: USE VIDEO GAIN WISELY

The advanced setting that you will probably use most is video gain. Video gain electronically brightens the darker areas of your picture.

As a rule, you want to apply as little video gain as possible. When you turn up gain, you also introduce noise into the video image. Noise shows up as "snow" or grain in the image.

Gain is a tradeoff—increased detail at the cost of increased noise.

Video gain tips

- You can apply gain at the camera or in your video editing program during postproduction. Given a choice, you want to apply gain in the camera rather than in post. Gain applied at the camera usually generates less noise than gain applied in the video editing program.

- Basically, you want to get as much detail in the shadows, and as few high-lights (blown) areas as possible. Of the two, it is more important to control the highlights, because people notice blown areas more than they do a lack of details in the shadows.
- Before you turn up the gain, look at the scene and think about ways you can get more light into the shadows without over-exposing the brighter areas in the scene. You might decide to shoot at a different time of day, bounce available light into the shadows, or use artificial light.
- You can use gain as an aesthetic tool. Some filmmakers like the "grainy" look of high gain, and deliberately turn up the gain to achieve that look.

SECRET 65: KNOW WHEN TO USE AUTOMATIC GAIN CONTROL (AGC)

AGC (Automatic Gain Control) tries to keep the sound at a certain level. Not too low, not too high.

Most of the time, this works pretty well. Especially in a situation like a wedding reception, where you have lots of background noise for the AGC to lock onto. AGC also keeps sound levels from going over limit when you have sudden loud sounds like clapping or cheering.

AGC works poorly in quiet places with occasional sound, like a quiet room. In a quiet room, AGC increases the gain during the quiet periods until the background noise in the room sounds like a "hiss."

AGC tips

- Turn AGC off when recording an interview in a quiet room.
- If you are recording on a busy street (lots of background noise), AGC will probably work fine.
- If you are recording something like Mozart's Overture to *The Marriage of Figaro* in a concert hall, AGC should be off. Set the recording level manually to a level where you can capture both the silence and the peaks of the music.
- Test your camcorder's recording capability before you shoot. Record something in an environment similar to the one where you will shoot. Record half with AGC on and half with AGC off. Write the results to a CD. Play the CD on a good stereo system to see which option works for you: AGC on or AGC off.

SECRET 66: UNDERSTAND FRAME RATES

Modern prosumer cameras often allow you to shoot at several different frame rates. Until very recently, the option of choosing a different frame rate was only something you would find on an expensive professional camera.

The frame rate options you are likely to see are:

Frame rate	What is it?	Format	When you might use it.
60i	North American standard for broadcast television.	NTSC*	You are going show your footage in North America, or sell it to a North American broadcaster. Converts to DVD easily.
50i	European standard for broadcast television.	PAL*	You are going to show your video in Europe or sell it to a European broadcaster. Converts to DVD easily.
30p	Non-standard frame rate. Available in some NTSC cameras.		You are going to web cast your footage, capture still frames, or watch it on a computer. Can be converted easily to standard 60i footage.
25p	Non-standard frame rate. Available in some PAL cameras.		You are going to convert your footage to 24 frames, capture still frames or watch it on your computer. Can be converted easily to standard 50i footage. Converts to DVD easily.
24p	Film	Worldwide standard for film (movies).	You are going to convert your footage to film, capture still frames, watch it on your computer, or create a DVD with a "film look."

* The most common standards are:
- NTSC: 30 frames (60 fields per second), 525 lines per frame.
- PAL: 25 frames (50 fields per second), 625 lines per frame.
- Film: 24 frames per second.

Standard shutter speeds for each frame rate

Each frame rate has a standard shutter speed that works well in many situations.

NTSC = 1/60 second.

PAL = 1/50 second.

24p = 1/48 second.

If you are shooting in low light and don't have enough light for a decent image, try reducing the standard shutter speed by ½.

NTSC = 1/30 second.

PAL = 1/25 second.

24p = 1/24 second.

Frame rate tips

- 60i is the most universally acceptable frame rate in North America.
- 50i is the most universally acceptable footage in Europe.
- France and several other countries use another 50i standard, SECAM.
- 24p looks more like film, and is the easiest frame rate to convert to film. For these reasons 24p is favored by many Directors of Photography on HD productions.
- 24p pans must be fairly slow or the footage will appear to "stutter."
- "Film out" is a process of taking video footage and converting it to film. Film out is a very complicated and expensive procedure. If you are considering film out, you might want to test the process before you begin production. Shoot a three-minute sample of video and send it to the conversion house to be converted to 35mm film. When your three-minute strip of film comes back, rent a movie theater and watch the sample.

SECRET 67: GAMMA SETTINGS

Gamma is an advanced setting that determines how a camera renders grayscales.

A few high-end prosumer cameras allow you to adjust the "gamma curve" of the video signal.

There are two common preset gamma curves: straight video gamma (TV), and some sort of film look. The best way to set gamma is to shoot some tests using the different preset gamma curves. Choose the look that suits your needs best.

If you intend to transfer your video to film, the best choice is to shoot with straight video gamma (TV). Straight video gamma will give you an image with less contrast than film look (cinegamma), but you can bump the contrast up in postproduction if necessary.

SECRET 68: CHANGING BLACK SETTINGS

Black is an advanced setting that changes the dynamic area within the black area of the video image.

Black stretch increases the dynamic range in the blackest areas of the image, enhancing the contrast within the black.

Black press reduces the dynamic range within the blackest area and the "blackness" of the black is deepened.

SECRET 69: USING SHARPNESS

Raising sharpness increases the sharpness of edges in the image. Decreasing the sharpness adjustment blurs the edges slightly.

A sharp edge shows up more than a "blurred" edge, especially during movement. If the edge is too sharp, the image may look "fake." Sharp, "hard" images are often associated with amateur home video and electronic news gathering.

Turning sharpness down will give the subjective appearance of a "softer" image with more detail. Soft images are traditionally associated with film.

Sharpness tip

- If you play back a video and it looks "too sharp," the problem may not be in your video, it may be in the monitor or television. Some people like the "sharp" look and turn their television's sharpness way up.
- 24p footage that is too sharp may appear to "strobe" when the camera moves.

SECRET 70: CHANGING THE SETUP LEVEL

Setup level is an advanced setting that changes the black level of the images. When setup level is increased, the shadow areas are brighter. When setup level is decreased, the whole image becomes darker.

When you adjust the setup level you can get more detail out of dark areas, often at the expense of detail in more brightly lit areas of the image.

Setup level tips

- Instead of playing with setup levels to get more detail in the dark areas, turn the camera gain up. You may be able to remove any gain-related noise in postproduction using something like NEAT VIDEO (an Adobe After Effects plug-in).
- The floor for setup level is determined by the master pedestal setting.

SECRET 71: UNDERSTAND MASTER PEDESTAL

Master pedestal is an advanced setting that adjusts the camera's black reference point.

Increasing master pedestal makes the dark areas of the image brighter, and overall contrast is reduced. Decreasing master pedestal makes the dark areas darker and overall contrast is increased.

SECRET 72: UNDERSTAND COLOR MATRIX

Color matrix is an advanced setting that controls the palette of colors that a camera generates.

Camera manufacturers design their camcorders to generate what they believe to be the optimal palette of colors for the camera's lens, imaging chip, and digital signal processor (DSP).

Adjusting the color matrix changes the factory settings for hue and saturation.

SECRET 73: UNDERSTAND KNEE

Knee is an advanced setting that changes the dynamic range of the brightest parts of the image.

Moving the knee higher increases the number of "blown" or overexposed areas in the image. Moving the knee lower tends to "protect the highlights" with fewer "blown" areas.

CHAPTER 10

SHOOTING IN COMMON SITUATIONS

You can learn to shoot in the most common situations.

The request sounds reasonable, and it usually comes from an acquaintance, family member or co-worker.

"We need someone to do a video of our event. We don't want much, just a record of the event. You don't have to do anything but shoot some footage and give us the tape afterward. We don't even want you to edit it."

Here's what this request really means:

We are looking for someone to shoot our event for free, and we expect the same quality of story, image, sound and editing that we see on the Hollywood movies that we rent for three dollars at the video store.

The best reply to this question is to smile sadly, shake your head slowly and say "I'm sorry, but I'm a really bad choice for taping the event."

SECRET 74: LEARN HOW TO SHOOT AN EVENT

When you shoot an event—whether it's a picnic or a poodle show—the main thing to remember is this: *the event dictates what and when you shoot.*

If you are shooting a traditional Midwestern family reunion, you could plan your shooting around the event activities: the arrival of Grandpa and Grandma, the softball game before dinner, and then the dinner. Afterwards, there's the cleaning of the table, the washing of the dishes, the football game on television and eventually everyone leaving for home.

Every event moves at a certain pace, with a beginning, a middle and an end.

The advantage of this is that you can plan your shooting around the general outline of the event. The disadvantage is that the event largely dictates what, when and where you will shoot. Often, you only get one chance to capture an image. If you miss the shot, it will be gone forever.

When you shoot an event, it helps to have a theme in mind. The theme need not be complicated. It might be something simple: "A record of this year's family reunion." Or it may be more complicated: "How our family sticks together when times are tough."

Having a theme in mind helps you decide on a plan for shooting. If you have a theme and a plan your shooting will go much more smoothly and your final show will be much more powerful.

Event tips

- Learn to use manual focus before you go to the event. Otherwise the camera will be "hunting" focus and much of your footage will be out of focus or blurred.
- Use the "push to focus" button to set focus just before each shot.
- If you are going to do any interviews, use an external microphone. Even an inexpensive microphone that you can hand to people will capture much better sound than the on-camera microphone.
- If your camera has manual white balance controls, use the appropriate white balance presets for each setting: outdoors, indoors and fluorescent. For a mixed lighting situation, set the initial white balance using "auto white balance." When white balance is set for the mixed light setting, turn auto white balance back to manual and leave it there as long as you are in that setting.
- If you are shooting in a brightly lit outdoors setting, use the ND filter to reduce the light.
- Get good candid shots. The trick to getting good candid shots is to have people forget you are there. The trick to making people forget you are there is to avoid eye contact and let situations unfold without joining in. Go with the flow, but don't be part of the flow. Have the camera ready.
- Learn your camera intimately before the event.
- Get physically close to people when shooting close-ups, and get plenty of close-ups of faces.
- Aim for a mix of long, medium, and close-up shots.
- Get "two shots" of people talking to each other.
- Try a monopod as a quick, easy way to stabilize your camera.

SECRET 75: LEARN HOW TO SHOOT IN THE RAIN

Rainy days tend to have a colorless, low key light. You may have to look for ways to add color to your videos. The source of color might be people walking by in brightly colored rain coats, lighted storefronts, flowers—anything.

On rainy days the "exterior" white balance setting may not be accurate, so you may want to use your white balancing card to set white balance manually.

A waterproof coat will work as a rain cover, but the sound of rain spattering on the jacket will ruin any sound recorded with the on-camera microphone.

Rain tips

- Raindrops are little lenses. If possible, find a way to backlight them to make them visible.
- Use rain-slick streets, puddles and reflections to add visual interest to your footage.

SECRET 76: **LEARN KNOW HOW TO SHOOT SPORTS**

The new, small high-definition camcorders are great for shooting sports. You can throw them in a pocket, or even mount them on a helmet.

You'll probably be shooting fast action, high-detail scenes outside. If so, use high shutter speeds to freeze action and avoid blur.

If bright sunlight overwhelms the camera, use the ND filter to reduce the light.

Sports tips

All the event shooting tips (the previous secret) apply equally to sporting events, but here are a few specific sports tips:

- A frame rate of 60i (for NTSC people) or 50i (for PAL people) is probably your best bet. Avoid 24p unless you are experienced in shooting 24p.
- Not all auto focus is created equal. Canon's "instant autofocus" is pretty good, and reacts very quickly. Experiment before the event. If your camera's auto focus responds quickly, shooting auto focus may be a good option for fast-moving action.
- Professional cameramen get slow motion sports shots by using high frame rates. A few inexpensive camcorders now have a high frame rate "super slo mo" option. If your camcorder has this option, you might want to experiment with it—before the sporting event—and find out what it can do for you.
- For sequential, detailed single frames of something like a golf swing, use a high shutter speed to freeze movement. Start at 1/250 and go up.

SECRET 77: **LEARN HOW TO SHOOT A PERFORMANCE**

Occasionally you may want to record a concert, speech or performance. The conditions are usually a dark seating area, and a well-lit stage. The performers are often lighted from the front with an even light that has little contrast.

Getting a good image in this situation is difficult at best.

If you put the camera on auto, you may get a mediocre image with severely "blown" highlights (bright areas of pure white with no detail).

To make the most of a bad situation try the following settings:
- Set the camera in manual mode.
- Turn viewfinder contrast up before you begin shooting, to make it easier to tell when you are in focus.
- Set white balance to tungsten.
- Readjust the aperture (iris) each time you refocus or move the camera.
- Start with the video gain at zero.
  Manually increase the gain to see if it improves the image, but do so carefully. If you turn the gain too high you will see noise in the shadows and blowouts in the brightly lit areas. If you use too little gain there will be no detail in the shadows.
  Get the best possible image while you are shooting, because you probably won't be able to "fix" it in post. Pulling detail out of very dark shadows or out of "blown" areas in post is impossible, because there is no detail there to begin with. You might be able to lighten the midrange areas in post, but doing so won't improve the image much.
- Set the zebras to 100, and adjust the iris until you see just a tiny bit of zebra stripes on the brightest parts of the image. (Zebra stripes won't record onto your image, they just tell you when something is overexposed.) You want to see a *tiny* bit of zebras here and there in your image. If you don't see *any* zebras, the image may be underexposed.
- Sound is usually a problem, because you are too far from the source of the sound to get good sound. An external directional microphone may help. In some situations, you might be able to record sound directly from the event's sound system.

SECRET 78: LEARN HOW TO SHOOT WEDDINGS

Begin planning your shoot well before the wedding. Start by getting an idea of what the final video is going to look like. You may even want to make a storyboard.

When you shoot a wedding, you are shooting something with a very predictable sequence. You can take advantage of this predictability when you plan your shoot.

Ideally, you want to go in with a plan and look for the images within the sequences that you need to fulfill your plan. If you go into the wedding without a clear idea of what you need, you may end up with three hours of video and a painful editing session as you try to create a video from the footage.

After the wedding, sit down and log all your footage.

Watch everything once, non-judgmentally. As you watch, keep a log and note the parts that are useful, good, and no good. Write down each part's time code so you can find it again.

When you have watched all the footage, plan your edit. The plan does not have to be too detailed, just a general outline. Then go back and pull the chunks you need from the footage and use them to create the first edit of the video.

Wedding tips

- Most weddings generally follow the same sequence: rehearsal, pre-ceremony, ceremony, reception, and post-reception. The sequence is so predictable that many wedding videographers develop templates that list all the shots they need for a wedding video. If you do a quick Internet search, you can probably find several such templates. They may give you some ideas for your own shooting plan.
- Once you start shooting, concentrate on getting the shots you need, and nothing else. You don't want to spend any more time in postproduction editing the footage than you have to. Shoot everything you need, but don't fall into the trap of shooting so much that you will be overwhelmed in postproduction.
- Try to begin every scene with a master shot (a wide shot of the entire scene). Once you have the master shot, shoot medium shots and close-ups. This protects you in two ways: it gives you a master shot to use in editing, and it helps you organize your footage.
- Stop the camera before each new setup. Stopping the camera before each setup breaks the clips into easy-to-organize chunks.
- Practice as much as you can with the camera before the wedding. You will shoot faster, and get better footage, if you are really familiar with your camera. When the wedding is happening, you won't have time to do anything but shoot.

Dramatic Filmmaking

The most important part of a dramatic film is the script. Without a great script, you are lost. The scripts of classic movies like *Blade Runner*, *Casablanca* and *Tender Mercies* are as compelling as well-written novels. Your script should be a compelling read, too.

For some reason beginning filmmakers often have this idea that the story will "work itself out" in production or in editing.

It won't.

One of the big problems with shooting an ultra-low budget feature is that people often go into it with a poor script and no appreciation for the importance of the story, or the difficulty of the project.

A seminar like the Dov Simens 2-Day Film School (*dovsimensfilmschool.com*) is worth checking out, if you are considering making a film. Simens talks frankly about scripts and goes on to give an excellent introduction to what's involved in bringing a script to the screen.

SECRET 79: THE BEST WAY TO LEARN HOW TO MAKE A FILM

Many filmmakers say that the best way to learn how to make a film is to make one. You might get a few friends together and shoot a ninety-minute "throw away" DV movie over a weekend. Don't have any expectations for the movie except getting the film done and making lots of mistakes.

SECRET 80: LEARN HOW TO SHOOT ON LOCATION

For most of us a "location" will be a room—in a house, store, garage or office building. The room may look great, but it was not designed for filmmaking. It's almost certain that you will have both sound and lighting problems.

Sound may be the most important technical thing on location. Bad sound will kill your movie faster than just about anything.

You should have a dedicated sound person who listens to all the sound. Then, you must listen to the sound person. If they ask you to readjust the lighting to remove the shadow of a boomed mike, then readjust the lighting. If they ask to have an air conditioner turned off, turn it off.

Mike (put a microphone on) all the actors individually. Ideally, you want to end up with a separate sound track for each actor. On that sound track should be the entire dialog of that actor.

Getting separate sound tracks for each actor may mean using boom microphones, wireless microphones, or hiding a microphone somewhere on the set.

While on the set, you need a way to tell immediately if your lighting works. In the long run the fastest, cheapest way to do this is to have a large monitor on set. Run the output of your camera to the monitor, and adjust the lighting until the monitor looks right. When the monitor looks right, the lighting is right.

Without a monitor, you are just guessing. The LCD on the camcorder is *not* a good indication of what the image will look like when the footage is shown on a high-definition TV or projected on a movie screen.

Tips for shooting on location

- Make a storyboard before you shoot.
- Don't try to do everything yourself. Doing everything yourself is possible, and people do it, but it's really, really tough.
- Scout the location before you shoot. Take a hand-held camera or a still camera and shoot images.
- Scout the location for sound. Listen for background noise, reverberation— anything that might mess up your sound track.
- Get a location release before you shoot.
- Watch your equipment. Things get stolen on location.
- When you pack up after shooting, have a checklist. It's easy to lose things in the confusion of packing up.
- Pay attention to safety. When people are making a film they are completely absorbed in what they are doing. Safety is a real concern, and you have to be aware of it at all times.
- Practice a short "pitch" that you can use with curious people. When a bystander asks, "What'cha doing?" have a friendly, simple, and boring answer ready. Something like, "I'm taking a film class and we're shooting a student film."
- Don't spend money unless you absolutely have to. Always look for a cheaper way to do things.

Documentary Filmmaking

The Irish farmer paused and looked across the valley. Several distant farmhouses gleamed in afternoon sunlight.

"We fought seven hundred years to return the land to the Irish, and it's going to be gone in two generations."

The farms are now owned by retirees from the European Union and the Irish farming families have moved to the cities. The farmer's quiet quote neatly described the disappearance of family farms in Ireland, and with them an entire way of life.

I got that quote, because I was ready to shoot "verite." I had not planned an interview with the farmer. We were on his farm shooting a reenactment of nineteenth-century farm life when he stopped, looked across the valley and began talking. I quickly lifted the camera and focused on his face. I got "wide and close" and got one of the best bits of footage in three weeks of shooting.

SECRET 81: LEARN HOW TO DO VERITE SHOOTING

Verite shooting, often with a small hand-held camera, is an informal style of shooting in which the shooter becomes a "fly on the wall."

It may be months before something happens that captures the dynamics of a situation. The verite shooter must be there when it happens. This requires an extraordinary amount of trust between the shooter and the people in the situation, and sensitivity to what is going on.

When shooting verite, always look for cutaways that reveal what Tom Wolfe calls the "status life" of the people being filmed. Indicators of "status life" are the possessions, activities, manners, and gestures that people use to indicate their place in their social situation.

Status life cutaways may be possessions: things like clothing, furniture, jewelry, cars, motorcycles, houses, cameras, paintings, or guns.

They may be bodily: tattoos, piercings, gestures, habitual facial expressions, dress, grooming or scars.

When you are shooting verite, you have to stay constantly aware and be ready for unplanned turns. When long-simmering resentment bursts into heated argument and a relationship is severed forever, the verite shooter must be there.

In all verite shooting, make sure—first of all—that you do not endanger yourself or others.

There are many ways to endanger others. The most obvious is when someone inadvertently reveals something on film that—if shown—might lead to severe consequences for the speaker or others.

SECRET 82: LEARN HOW TO GAIN ACCESS AND BUILD TRUST

Two keys to all documentary filmmaking are access and trust.

Access often comes through a "gatekeeper." A gatekeeper is someone who controls access to an individual or a community.

Formal gatekeepers may work as secretaries, administrative assistants, or public relations professionals. They are paid to screen people out.

Informal gatekeepers are generally individuals within a community who are known, respected and trusted by the members of the group.

Once you have access to a person or a community, you have to build trust. Some of the best documentary filmmakers have the knack of establishing trust immediately. Some say that they can do it with eye contact alone—within a few seconds of meeting someone. The rest of us may need weeks, months, or even years to build the degree of trust required for good documentary filmmaking.

SECRET 83: PUT YOURSELF IN THE FILM

Documentary filmmakers have a long tradition of being a character in their own films.

Before using yourself in the film, ask yourself, "Am I a major character in this story?" Look at yourself as a character, just as you would look at any other character. Only if you are a major character, should you consider putting yourself in the story.

Filmmaker Ross McElwee did just this in his classic documentary *Sherman's March*. His film was about more than retracing General Sherman's route during the Civil War; the film was also about McElwee's relationships with women. Thus McElwee was a major character in the story he was telling.

If you film yourself, the best thing is to have a cameraman. However, there are a couple of tricks you can use if you are shooting alone:

- Shoot into a mirror, and let the audience watch you in the mirror, as you hold the camera and talk to them.
- Stand in front of the camera and speak. Put the camera on a support and focus on the spot where you will be standing. Press Record, and step in front of the camera.
- Use a hand-held microphone. Try something simple like holding a wired lavaliere microphone in your hand. Keep the microphone close to your mouth.

SECRET 84: LEARN HOW TO SHOOT INTERVIEW FOOTAGE

Interviews are a significant part of most documentaries.

You need three things for a good interview: candor, good sound and good facial lighting.

The interviewee must trust you before you will get candor.

Sometimes you do not need a long period of trust-building. For instance, when you have been introduced by a trusted gatekeeper, or when your interviewee has a message to get out to the world.

Once the interview begins, follow the interviewee's enthusiasm. Listen to the interviewee's tone of voice and watch body language. When you sense enthusiasm, gently encourage the interviewee to expand upon the topic.

Have questions prepared in advance, but allow the interview to take its own course within the bounds of the subject you are discussing. Think of the interview as a river. You float along the river, but stay within the banks of the river. Occasionally, however, a side stream appears and your boat is swept out of the river.

When your interviewee leads you into a side stream, sometimes you go with the flow and allow the interviewee to reveal an aspect of the subject that you did not know existed before. You can get some of your best interview footage this way.

Depending on the acoustic quality of the spaces where you will be interviewing, you may need more than one microphone. You may also need a separate audio mixer to mix the outputs of the microphones.

If you can't hire a professional sound person, at least ask a professional for advice. Then, run some tests and see which microphones work for you.

Here are a few basic guidelines for facial lighting in interviews:
The first guideline is to look for sparkle in the eyes. If there's not enough light reaching the eyes to make them sparkle, they will appear dark and lifeless on the screen.

The second guideline is to use a soft light. A soft light will make faces look appealing and lively. Soft light comes from north-facing windows (in the northern hemisphere), or filtered lights like Chinese lanterns or lights with diffusion material in front of them. Do not light your faces with the harsh light of direct, mid-day sunlight, or the light coming through a south-facing window. Such light will make the interviewee's face look aged and wrinkled.

The third is a lighting ratio of 4:1. The light should fall gently across the face with the difference in amount between the brightest spots and darkest spots of about 4:1. A lighting ratio of 4:1 is about two f-stops difference. Less than 4:1 gives a flat image. More gives a high contrast image.

CHAPTER 11

SHOOTING IMAGES THAT HAVE MEANING

How do you capture an image with meaning?

The hardest thing to do is to shoot an image that has meaning.

When an image has meaning it "gets under your skin" and lodges itself somehow in people's minds.

I recently tested this. I asked a dozen people the question, "Do you remember the picture of the Afghan woman?"

Everyone said yes. They didn't need any additional information to recall photographer Steve McCurry's haunting photograph of a young Afghan woman.

Certain film scenes have the same power. The ones that come to my mind immediately are the opening scene from *The Godfather*, the closing scene in *Casablanca*, and the scenes with the girl in the red coat in *Schindler's List*.

Every person can recall a few images from real life that have the same power. These images are as unique and individual as our lives. You can probably recall a few of your own. These images are profoundly intimate, and we never forget them.

One of mine is of wild strawberries growing next to a country road. The vivid red surface of each berry is covered with light brown dust, in the stillness of a hot Ohio summer afternoon, half a century ago.

Another: A red Corvette sports car skids out of control, directly toward the car I am riding in. Suddenly time seems to slow down. The phrase, "This is what it is like to die," goes through my mind. (The sports car struck a glancing blow, causing minor damage to both cars.)

Such images are unique in their emotional power. They are somehow different than other images; they have *meaning*.

An image with meaning is not the same as an image that arouses your interest. An image without much meaning may capture interest for the moment—like the images on the daily news, or in an average movie.

We may be profoundly interested in such images at the moment, but we forget them soon afterward. However, images with meaning have a way of lodging themselves in people's minds.

How do you capture an image with meaning?

There is no formula for capturing such images on film or digital video. However, there are a few things that you can do that will increase your chances of capturing such images.

SECRET 85: BE IN THE RIGHT PLACE AT RIGHT TIME, AND BE PREPARED

Louis Pasteur once observed that "In the field of observation, chance favors the prepared mind."

Again and again, photographers and filmmakers talk about how they captured extraordinary images because they took the time and effort to place themselves in situations where they were likely to have an opportunity to capture such images.

It may mean sitting in the field and waiting an extra five minutes for the light to change and getting a shot that no one else will get.

Or it may mean letting the camera run after an interview is "over." Suddenly the interviewee looks up and says, "You know, I wasn't going to say anything, but...."

In each case the filmmaker was *ready* for the moment. After months or years of practice, the filmmaker finds him or herself in the right place, at the right time, with the right tools, and the right skills.

SECRET 86: HAVE A TECHNICAL MASTERY OF THE CRAFT

In *Story: Substance, Structure, Style and the Principles of Screenwriting*, Robert McKee writes that "Anxious, inexperienced writers obey rules. Rebellious, unschooled writers break rules. Artists master the form."

Great filmmakers—the ones who capture extraordinary images consistently— have a profound mastery of the craft of filmmaking.

They make it their business to become experts in all of the technical aspects of filmmaking.

They study the mechanics of filmmaking. They watch films by other filmmakers. They say things like, "I watched that film ten times to see how he got those images."

SECRET 87: LEARN TO SEE THINGS ANEW

Robert Bresson had this to say about freshness of perception. "Make visible what, without you, might never have been seen."

Painter Georgia O'Keeffe was able to make her amazing paintings of flowers because she saw them anew. As filmmakers, we too must take time to see things as if for the first time.

When you slow down and really take time to look at a scene, or a person, or a flower, you see what is really there.

If you are lucky, you will see things freshly, and your preconceptions will fall away. You may discover the unexpected in the commonplace. If you are both skilful and patient, you may be able to capture this image, and challenge the preconceptions of others.

Learn to see things anew.

SECRET 88: **GET CLOSE**

Sometimes the difference between capturing a meaningful image and a meaningless one is as simple as getting the camera close to someone's face. Audiences love intimate close-ups of faces. Close-ups reveal a person's character.

Get the camera physically close to the person and use the widest angle lens practical. When you open your lens, don't go so wide that the facial features are distorted, but go as wide as you can.

SECRET 89: TELL A STORY

"The world now consumes films, novels, theatre, and television in such quanti-
ties and with such ravenous hunger that the story arts have become humanity's
prime source of inspiration as it seeks to order chaos and gain insight into life,"
writes Robert McKee in *Story: Substance, Structure, Style and the Principles of
Screenwriting.*

Always tell a story.

When you are shooting digital video, ask yourself two questions. What story am I
telling? Why would my audience care?

These are difficult questions. Don't be discouraged if finding the story within your
project is the hardest thing you do. It's that way for everyone. The story is the most
elusive and frustrating part of filmmaking.

If you are serious about learning about story, you might want to read Robert McKee's
book *Story: Substance, Structure, Style and the Principles of Screenwriting.*

Another way to learn about story is to deconstruct well-written films.

For this exercise, you will watch the film four times.
1. The first time watch the film with the sound on. Enjoy the movie, and don't
   analyze anything.
2. Next, watch it with the sound off. Watch the editing, and see how the images
   are assembled to tell a story.
3. The third time, turn the image off and listen to the sound track. Get a feel
   for how the script is crafted, and how the movie was written.
4. The fourth time, watch the movie shot by shot. Press the pause button after
   each shot. Make a note of how the shot was done, and the shot's purpose.

If you are planning on making a film, you might find a similar film—in length,
budget, subject, and content—and deconstruct it. See if you can learn how the
filmmakers solved the problems you are about to face.

SECRET 90: TELL THE TRUTH

The seventeenth-century French mathematician and philosopher Blaise Pascal observed that "We know the truth, not only by the reason, but also by the heart."

In all that you do, try to show what is true about the person, place, or thing that you are shooting.

You may see the truth of a situation in an intuitive flash of insight or you might learn the truth of a situation through patient research and observation. Filmmakers have been known to spend weeks, months and occasionally years living in a place to learn its reality.

When we first look at a scene, we all have the tendency to allow it to order itself in our minds in a conventional way. Any images we shoot at this point will reflect this conventional vision. Most likely, the images will be bland and uninteresting.

One way to break out of conventional vision is to slow down. Allow yourself time to observe a scene. You will slowly begin to get a sense of the images which might communicate the truth of what you see.

SECRET 91: KEEP IT MEANINGFUL TO YOU

Images that don't mean anything to you will not mean anything to the audience. The first person that has to care about the image is you.

When you care about the image you see it in a different way. You may see it in a way that no one else sees it. Your subsequent shots will have a freshness and aliveness that will captivate audiences.

Apply your skills of composition, color selection and framing to the image. Employ your craftsmanship to communicate what you feel.

SECRET 92: HAVE COMPELLING, INTERESTING CHARACTERS

Director John Frankenheimer once said, "Casting is 65% of directing."

One of the most powerful things you can do to create compelling footage is to have a compelling, interesting character.

Finding a compelling character is so important that a documentary filmmaker may interview hundreds of people before choosing one person as the central character for a film.

Likewise, independent filmmakers may audition hundreds of people before choosing actors for their films.

Always tape auditions and interviews and don't make any decisions before you watch the footage. An actor or character that you found bland and uncommunicative in person might be fascinating on film.

You just can't tell who will "come through the screen" until you watch the tape. Wait a couple of days after the audition or interview before you watch your footage. Your impressions will be fresher, and you will be rested. You will be surprised at how differently the actors come across on film compared to your memory of them.

CHAPTER 12

CHOOSING THE BEST CAMERA FOR YOU

What is your dream?

What is your dream?

I have come to believe that cameras represent dreams. They represent dreams of starting a business, making a film, or capturing the first steps of the new son or daughter. Or they are dreams of recording a once-in-a-lifetime vacation in vivid, beautiful detail.

It's hard to be objective about dreams.

But, before we choose a camera we have to find a way to be objective about our dreams. We have to ask ourselves these questions.

- What is this camera going to be used for, really?
- How much can I afford, really?
- Does this camera feel good in my hands?
- Do I like the image this camera produces?

This chapter is an attempt to help you answer those questions, and hopefully to save you some time and money along the way.

I have a hard time buying a camera. I'll read the Internet forums for months, read specifications, handle cameras at the camera store, agonize for days and finally make a choice.

Then I usually spend the next two years worrying about whether I bought the right camera. Because the minute I buy the camera, a newer, better, and cheaper version comes out.

After buying a dozen cameras I finally learned how to tell when a camera is out of date. I now know that a camera is obsolete the moment I open the box.

I now accept the fact that cameras change so rapidly, and new features come along so quickly, that there's no way anyone can keep up.

Instead of trying to find the perfect, most up-to-date camera I have learned that it's better to just get going with my project and use the camera that I have.

SECRET 93: THE CAMERA DOESN'T MATTER

Photographer Ken Rockwell's opinion is that "it's entirely an artist's eye, patience and skill that makes an image and not his tools." (See *www.kenrockwell.com/tech/notcamera.htm* for details.)

Just about any MiniDV camera can capture images that are good enough to make a feature length documentary or film—one that will be technically good enough to win prizes at film festivals.

All of the films listed in the beginning of the book were made with three-chip prosumer or one-chip consumer DV cameras.

Each of these films has a good story, compelling characters, a unique vision, decent production values and good sound. *The specific camera really doesn't matter that much.*

Does this mean you should just grab any camera for your production? Of course not. You should still do everything possible to get your hands on the best camera for the job. All it means is that there are other things more important than any specific camera.

Some of them are:
- Story
- Acting
- Sound
- The people behind the camera
- Production values
- Postproduction

Beginning and first-time filmmakers have a tendency to fixate on cameras. This might be a way to avoid the more difficult and scary task of making movies.

SECRET 94: DON'T GET CAUGHT IN THE NUMBERS GAME

You can drive yourself crazy on the Internet comparing the features, pixel counts, resolution tests, and costs of different cameras.

This is known as getting caught in the numbers game.

If you are caught in the numbers game, stop! Just stop.

Make your best bet on a camera, buy it and start shooting. You will not only have fun shooting, but you will gain valuable experience for your next camera purchase.

Every camera has its strengths and weaknesses. There is no one best camera, and no perfect camera. Every camera has flaws and every camera has strengths.

SECRET 95: BE CLEAR ABOUT WHAT YOU REALLY NEED IN A CAMERA

Surprisingly, many people buy cameras without taking an hour or so to think through what they really need the camera for, and what they want the camera to do for them.

Let's look at some of the common uses for cameras.

Film student cameras

There's a lot to be said for owning your own camera when you are in film school. In most film schools the school cameras get knocked about badly, and many of them have minor problems.

The cameras available to beginning film students are usually the worst of the bunch. The best cameras are restricted to the advanced students. If you buy your own camera, you can shoot any time you want—on any project you choose.

You may not need a three-chip camera. A durable one-chip camera—especially if it is one of the new HD cameras—may be sufficient. When you shoot your final project, you can rent a good three-chip camera.

Your camera should have as many manual controls as you can afford so you can experiment with as many camera options as possible.

It should be rugged. When you are in film school you will use the camera a lot—maybe several times a week for a couple of years.

The camera will probably get knocked about a fair amount, so you also need a sturdy carrying case. With a good case, you can safely take the camera on student film shoots. When you go home for the summer, you'll use the case to haul your camera home.

Occasionally, you can save money by buying a used prosumer camera. Look for last year's top-of-the-line prosumer camera and buy it from someone who bought the camera with all the attachments and a carrying case.

A good place to find such kits is the bulletin board at film school. When teachers upgrade equipment they often sell their old stuff to a student.

Independent filmmaker cameras

Independent filmmakers don't really use their cameras very often. The number of shooting days in a year may only be ten or twenty. The rest of the year or two that it takes to make an independent film is often spent doing preproduction (planning and preparing) and postproduction (editing and marketing).

When you are only going to use a camera for twenty days a year, one approach is to rent a high-end camera for those few days.

You may not feel comfortable operating a complicated high-end camera. A good option is to hire a cameraperson. Many camera operators own very good three-chip cameras and are quite skilled with them. For the day rate that you pay the camera operator, you get not only the camera, but all the accessories, experience and skills that you need to capture top quality images.

If you decide to buy instead of rent, do some research and find out which camera fits your needs. Before you buy the camera, you should at least watch one film that was shot with the camera you are considering. Do an Internet search and see if the camera person gave any interviews about shooting the film.

The camera rig needed to shoot an independent film can be quite bulky and heavy. You may decide to mount the camera on a heavy tripod or on a Steadicam system. Your camera person may want to attach rails (rods that extend forward beneath the lens), matte boxes (to hold filters), flags (to shield the lens from stray light), or a specialized viewfinder.

If you decide to rent a good camera for two weeks, you may want your own camera for the remaining fifty weeks of the year. Think of your own camera as a "daily" camera that you can use for location scouting, interviewing, and auditions.

Depending on your budget, you might consider a low-end prosumer three-chip camcorder, or a high-end one-chip consumer camera with manual controls.

The Film Look

If you want film look, you probably want a camera with some sort of 24-frame capability and the ability to choose different gamma curves. You may want a camera with an extremely good lens and as many manual controls as possible.

For the ultimate film look (shallow depth of field), you will need a camera that will accept a 35mm adapter. 35mm adapters from companies like Cinevate and Redrock Micro allow you to use high-end 35mm lenses with your digital video camera.

What most people think of as film look is a high-resolution, high-budget aesthetic. The camera is only a small part of this aesthetic. The film look is really a combination of 35mm film, story, acting, directing, cinematography, art direction, and exquisite sound.

When an edited 35mm film is transferred to DVD, the transfer is done by talented people using expensive hardware and software to get the ideal sound and image.

There's a reason the list of credits are so long on Hollywood films.

No camera is likely to replace the millions of dollars, dozens of people and years of experience that it takes to conceive and produce a high-resolution Hollywood film which embodies the film look aesthetic.

Documentary filmmaker cameras

People who make documentaries use their cameras a lot. They may use them daily for months, in all sorts of weather. Often a documentary filmmaker will have to cross borders with the camera, or pack it in a backpack. A camera that is small, rugged, and simple is a distinct plus.

Appearance counts with a documentary camera. You might want to look for a prosumer camera that looks like a cheap consumer camera.

The advantages of a smaller camera are several. You may find it easier to slip the camera into your pocket and carry it with you. Having a camera with you at all times, you might get shots you'd otherwise not get.

You may be able to use a small camera in places where "no press or media are allowed." With a large conspicuous camera on your shoulder, you might get thrown out.

You may not need a camera with interchangeable lenses to shoot a documentary. In most situations, modern zoom lenses will get the job done.

One accessory that is almost essential for a fixed-lens camera is a screw-on wide angle adapter. A wide angle adapter allows you to get wide and close to your subject in small spaces.

For the best possible sound quality, look for a camera with built-in XLR (three-pin) connectors that will allow you to use professional microphones. As a general rule, cameras with built-in XLR audio connectors will have better audio circuits than cameras that only have mini-stereo audio connectors.

Event videographer cameras

If you are an event videographer, your camera is a business tool. You will be shooting week in and week out. You need a camera that is first of all dependable.

You might consider buying last year's hot camera. Six months or a year after a camera's introduction, thousands of cameramen have used the camera in all kinds of shooting situations. Their feedback is often incorporated into version 2.0 of a new camera.

Occasionally, size matters. As an event videographer, you may find that your clients want to see a large "professional-looking" camera on your shoulder when you arrive for a job. One way to get a read on this is to find out what cameras your competition is using. If they are all using full-size shoulder-mount cameras, there's a good chance that you might want to consider getting the same type.

SECRET 96: FIND A CAMERA THAT FEELS RIGHT TO YOU

The best camera is one that feels like an extension of your hand and eye. A camera that feels right in your hands will get used more often, and you will be more enthusiastic about your shooting.

When you have done all your research and limited your cameras to one or two models, visit a camera store and try them out.

When you buy a camera, buy from a reputable vendor, one that allows you to exchange your purchase. If the camera doesn't feel right, you can return it and try another model. Don't try to talk yourself into making a camera feel right. If it doesn't feel right, it isn't right for you.

SECRET 97: LOOK AT THE FOOTAGE ON A GOOD MONITOR

The other important thing about choosing a camera is how the output looks on a monitor. Every camera's image is slightly different. Some people love Canon's look and wouldn't think of buying anything else. Other people love Sony's look. Still others like JVC or Panasonic. There is no right or wrong, only what you like.

SECRET 98: KNOW HOW TO ESTIMATE THE REAL COST OF THE CAMERA

Make sure you include the cost of accessories when you estimate the cost of the camera. The basic accessories are:

Tripod
Microphone(s)
Wind screens for microphones
Cables for microphones
UV filter
Polarizing filter
Carrying case
Extra battery
Extra media

The accessory worksheet at the end of this chapter lists accessories you might consider.

A good way to get an idea of the kind of accessories you might need is to look at the camera on the B&H Photo and Video website *(www.bhphotovideo.com)*. B&H has a comprehensive list of accessories for each camera that they sell.

Don't buy a prosumer camera in March. The annual NAB (National Association of Broadcasters) convention is in April, and that's when all the new cameras are announced, along with price reductions on last year's cameras.

SECRET 99: AVOID CAMERA SCAMS

Camcorders are a big-ticket item, and big-ticket items attract scam artists. The best way to avoid scams is to buy everything from a reputable vendor.

Be extremely careful if you buy a camera through an online auction site. Be sure you read the scam guides, and the site's guidelines for online purchases.

Beware super-low prices on the Internet. Often these prices are "bait and switch," con games. When you call about the camera, the salesman will try to sell you a lot of expensive accessories and warranties. If you refuse the extras, the camera is suddenly "not available." Such cameras may come without warranties, manuals, or accessories, and may be damaged. You will probably be stuck with the camera, and unable to return it.

Remember, when it comes to price: If it sounds too good to be true, it probably is.

SECRET 100: KNOW THE COMMON CONSUMER FORMATS

The common formats used in consumer and prosumer cameras are:

Format	Thumbnail description	Aspect ratio*	Resolution**
MiniDV	High-quality SD (standard definition) digital video. Uses small, inexpensive tape cassettes.	4:3	480i
DVCAM	Sony format, a professional version of DV. Uses same cassette as MiniDV, but tape runs 50% faster for more reliable recording.	4:3	480i
DVCPRO	Panasonic format, a professional version of DV. DVCPRO designed for higher reliability, easier editing and better audio. Uses special Panasonic designed tape.	4:3	480i
HDV	HD (high definition) on a standard MiniDV tape cassette. Widely used standard. Supported by many editing packages.	16:9	720p 1080i
AVCHD	Highly compressed HD with potentially higher quality than HDV. Digital video often recorded to memory cards, hard disk or DVD-R memory.	16:9	720p 1080i
DVCPRO-HD	Panasonic HD format. Industry standard with high quality, wide editing package support, and a robust signal. Records to Panasonic designed tape, P2 solid state cards, or hard disk.	16:9	720p, 1080i

* 16:9 is the widescreen format of the future. Most high-definition television screens are 16:9 format.
** The number of lines used to fill a television screen once, from top to bottom every 1/30 second. Generally, higher is better than lower and progressive is better than interlaced. 480i=480 lines, interlaced scan. 720p=720 lines, progressive scan. 1080i = 1080 lines, interlaced scan.

SECRET 101: **KNOW THE COMMON FRAME RATES**

Different parts of the world use different broadcast standards for video. The frame rates of these video standards are different. The main thing you need to remember when buying a camera is this:

NTSC cameras: 60i

PAL cameras: 50i

Film look: 24p.

NTSC is the broadcast standard used in the United States, Canada, Japan, Mexico, South Korea, Taiwan, the Philippines and many other countries.

PAL is a broadcast standard used by over 120 countries. Many of them are in Europe, the Middle East, and Southeast Asia.

If you are living in an NTSC area, there is no reason to buy a PAL camera unless you intend to convert the PAL signal to film (24p), or if you intend to sell your show in PAL countries.

Some cameras allow you to switch between PAL, NTSC, and 24p.

PAL signals will not play on NTSC televisions and vice versa.

SECRET 102: **CHOOSE A FORMAT WITH ENOUGH RESOLUTION**

How much resolution is enough? Nobody knows. There are several possible HD standards out there, and no one even knows (2008) what the standard for HD DVDs will be.

Going by the flat screen televisions that arrived in television stores this year, the resolution that everyone seems to be fixating on is 1080p (1080 lines, 60-frame progressive.)

What does this mean for us as filmmakers? Nobody knows. There isn't a widely used, agreed-upon standard yet for broadcast HD or for high-definition DVDs, so we have no "standard" to shoot for. So what do we do?

If we choose the wrong format, all our shows could end up in the same bin as VHS a few years from now.

I'm going to go out on a limb and make some guesses.

1. If I wanted to absolutely "future proof" my next film, and I had the budget, I'd find a way to shoot 1080p in 16x9 aspect ratio.

   The only reasonable way I know to shoot and archive 1080p today is the Sony XDCAM series. (Competing cameras from other manufacturers will probably appear by the time you read this.) SonyXDCAMs are designed to write their 1080p footage directly to special Sony DVDs.

   XDCAMs also write to hard disks and flash memory, but I wouldn't personally archive my footage to a hard disk. I don't trust hard disks as a long-term (years) archive medium.

2. My choice for an inexpensive high-definition format would be HDV. The cameras are inexpensive, and HDV tapes are cheap and plentiful. The HDV format is so popular that I'm pretty sure that I will be able to play and edit an HDV show in five years. The resolution of HDV is high enough that the image looks great on a fifty-inch flat screen.

SECRET 103: LOOK FOR A CAMERA WITH A MICROPHONE JACK

One input you should probably look for on any camera you buy is a microphone-in jack. With a microphone-in jack, you can use external microphones to record sound while you are shooting.

There are two kinds of microphone jacks: XLR and mini-jacks.

Three-pin XLR jacks are the standard for all professional microphones. Only pro-sumer and high-end cameras have XLR jacks for microphones.

Mini jacks are generally used for consumer-grade microphones. Sometimes, a consumer-grade microphone may be all you need. If you are careful in microphone placement and record in a setting which has little noise or reverberation, the sound may be perfectly acceptable.

If you decide that you need to use professional (XLR) microphones on a camera with a mini jack, you can add an after-market XLR adapter like the ones from BeachTek. Some people even like the BeachTek adapters better than built-in XLR connectors.

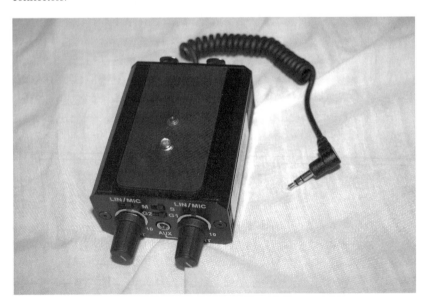

With a BeachTek XLR adapter, the XLR connectors are moved under the camera and you get two large knobs to control the sound level.

The second input you might want to look for is a headphone jack. Someone needs to be listening to the sound while you are recording. An XLR adapter usually has a headphone jack. If your camera doesn't have a headphone jack that's another reason to consider an XLR adapter.

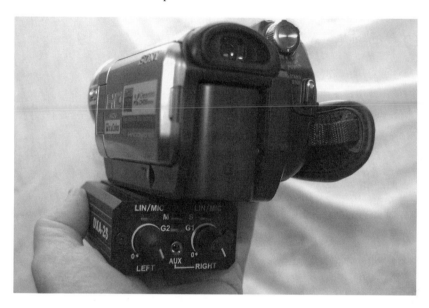

Lenses are crucial when you are shooting HD. Images shot with good lenses have extraordinary clarity. The whole image is in focus, right out to the edges of the picture.

Unlike electronics, lens costs are largely irreducible. Electronics and flash memory keeps getting cheaper, but no one has figured out how to significantly reduce the cost of a high-quality lens. Canon is a good example. They tend to put expensive lenses on their cameras. When you spend $5,000 for a Canon HD camera, $3,000 of that cost may be for the lens. If you buy a $700 HD camera, you won't get a lens of this quality.

The best way to check lens quality is to shoot test images of a high resolution test chart. (You can find such charts on the Internet.)

If you don't have a test chart, here are three things to look for that will help you make a quick guess at the quality of a lens.

Remember, though, there is no such thing as a perfect lens. Chances are that the lens on *any consumer camera* will have all of these problems to a greater or lesser degree. The question is, can you live with it?

Breathing. A lens is said to breathe when the apparent focal length of the lens changes as you change the mechanical focus of the lens. To test for breathing, zoom in and focus on a detail in the scene. Then, zoom back out. The item should stay in focus all the way back out. If the lens breathes, the item will go out of focus.

Vignetting. A lens is said to have vignetting when the amount of light reaching the edges of the image is less than the light in the center of the image. Open the lens all the way up, and check to see if the edges of the image, especially the corners, are dimmer than the center. Sometimes you can eliminate vignetting by reducing the aperture by two or three f-stops.

Barrel distortion. A lens is said to have barrel distortion when the image appears slightly "inflated." To test for barrel distortion, open a zoom lens as wide as it will go. Take a picture of something with verticals on each edge, like a doorway. If the lens has barrel distortion, the vertical edges of the doorway will appear to bow out. (Most zoom lenses have this at the extreme wide angle; it's a question of what you can live with.) The greater the degree of "bowing out," the greater degree of barrel distortion. You may be able to fix barrel distortion in postproduction.

SECRET 104: GET AS MANY MANUAL CONTROLS AS YOU CAN AFFORD

You want as many manual controls as possible, preferably at a minimum:
Zoom
White Balance
Shutter Speed
Iris
Focus
Microphone Level (audio input)

SECRET 105: UNDERSTAND YOUR CAMERA'S WORKFLOW

With the digital revolution in video, came a new term: workflow.

Workflow is the term for postproduction processing of the image. Before you choose a digital video camera, learn what computer and software you will need to edit the output.

The major video editing packages are constantly evolving. Manufacturers of editing packages are adding new formats and editing capabilities as fast as they can.

Before you buy a camera, check the Internet discussion groups and see what people are saying about editing the output of the camera. Make sure there are no major software problems that will stop your editing in mid-stride.

Find out what type of computer you need to edit the signal. Some of the HD formats require a fairly substantial computer.

While you are at it, find out if you need special hardware to get the footage into your computer. Ideally you want to be able to transfer your signal directly to the computer via firewire cable, USB cable or by plugging a memory card into a slot on your computer.

SECRET 106: LOOK FOR A CAMERA WITH A SUPPORT INFRASTRUCTURE

Popular, well-built cameras can quickly develop a large and passionate group of users. These users love to talk about their cameras, and they love to help beginners solve camera problems.

These people, plus any books, DVDs or manufacturer support, are what I call the "support infrastructure" for a camera.

When you find a camera with a good support infrastructure, you can find answers to camera questions quickly.

Look for a camera for which you can find:
- Internet forums devoted to the camera
- Books
- DVDs
- Manufacturer support

About Internet forums

Cameras with active Internet communities give you access to the expertise of thousands of people.

A good place to start your search for such an Internet community is DVinfo.net (*http://dvinfo.net*).

The first step is to see if your camera has a forum on DVinfo.net. The complete list of forums on Dvinfo.net is at *http://dvinfo.net/conf/*.

Next, you might Google the camera's name and see if any other forums pop up. For example, when I Googled the phrase *Canon HV20 forums* I found the HV20 forum at *http://www.hv20.com/*.

Books and DVDs are important too. Go on Amazon and search for the camera, and see if you can find any how-to books for it.

While you are on Amazon, you may also want to search for DVDs that explain the camera.

SECRET 107: TECHNICAL SUPPORT

The first place I turn for technical support information these days is an Internet discussion group like DVinfo.net. I start by doing a quick search of the forums to see if anyone else has reported the problem that I'm having. If I can't find an answer, I post a question to the group and see what comes up.

Always double-check the information you get on the Internet. Most of the time Internet discussion groups are both knowledgeable and helpful, but occasionally you'll get an answer that is just plain wrong.

Manufacturer technical support is critical

Good technical support is both difficult and expensive. As a result, manufacturer technical support only works when there's a real commitment from the manufacturer.

How to evaluate a manufacturer's technical support.

1. Do an Internet search of the camera's discussion group. Look for a pattern of comments about how the manufacturer responds to problems. Ignore the occasional flame or rant. Look instead for a general pattern in the comments.

2. Look at the manufacturer's website. If they have a serious commitment to technical support, you will probably see things like:
   - Recent white papers on technical subjects.
   - A comprehensive and regularly updated FAQ.
   - Downloads of new releases of software and firmware.
   - Contact information. It should be easy to reach tech support.

3. Look for the names of the manufacturer's technical support people and product managers in the camera forums. The best product managers and support people are often very active in their camera's Internet discussion forums. This is a very good sign of excellent support.

4. Call or email tech support with a test question and see how quickly they get back to you.

CHAPTER 13

ASSEMBLING THE IDEAL KIT FOR YOU

A video kit is more than a camera. It is the camera and all the accessories you need to get good images and good sound.

We all tend to think of the "kit" as the cost of the camera. My experience, however, has been that the camera is only half of the kit. Whatever the camera costs, add that much again to get an idea of how much a finished kit should cost.

To write this chapter, I assembled four video kits. The cost of the kits ranges from $0 to $7,800.

Zero dollars? Unbelievably, you can assemble a video kit for nothing.

No-budget video kits

You can assemble a video kit for (almost) no money. Here are a few ways that people have done so in the past:

- Borrow a friend or relative's video camera and start shooting. Edit the footage at your local public television station, or on a borrowed computer. Post it on YouTube, or burn a couple DVDs and you are done.

- Take a class at the local community college and use the school's cameras and computers to shoot and edit your film.
- If you are lucky enough to have a local not-for profit filmmaking organization in your city, contact them. In the San Francisco Bay Area, two such

organizations are San Francisco Film Society (*http://www.sffs.org*) and Bay Area Video Coalition (*www.bavc.org*). Organizations like these sometimes offer filmmaking classes, grants, seminars, and equipment rentals.

- Hook up with other "no-budget" filmmakers and exchange services. You might find someone who has a camera but needs your writing skills or acting skills. You might write his or her script and act in the film, and in exchange, he or she might shoot and edit your film. A lot of this sort of exchange goes on in the independent film world. The trick is to find the people, and to become known as someone who is trustworthy and reliable. Be scrupulously honest in all your dealings. *Always do what you promise to do!*

For more information on how to successfully produce a no-budget film and work with people in the independent film world, see my previous book, *Producing with Passion*. In that book my co-author, Oscar-nominated, Emmy-winning filmmaker Dorothy Fadiman, and I explain exactly how we have done both these things for the last thirty years!

Very low-budget video kit

1. FLIP Ultra video camera, $149 from B and H Photo (*www.bhphotovideo.com*).
2. Travel tripod, $15 at local discount store.
3. Logitech premium Notebook Headset $60 from Logitech (*www.logitech.com*). (The headset and microphone are for listening to audio on your computer, and possibly for recording narration.)
4. 2 AA batteries, $2.
5. Camera bag (not shown), $24 at local discount store.

Extra media: None. (Camera has built-in solid-state memory.)

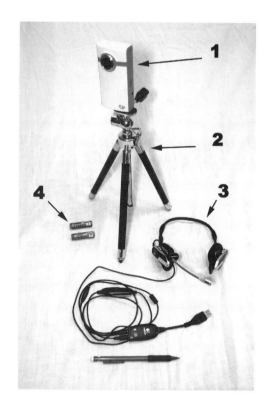

Lights: None. (Shoot in brightly lit places.)
Computer: Inexpensive Windows laptop, borrowed from a friend.
Editing software: Windows Movie Maker (included with Windows).
Sound recording and editing software: Total Sound Recorder from High Criteria (*www.highcriteria.com*), free download.
Total cost: $250.

Comments

You can easily throw this whole kit into a small camera bag and carry it with you everywhere.

The FLIP camera is easy to use. There are only two controls: an on-off button, and a big red record button. The video quality is excellent for low-resolution online posting on sites like YouTube. The camera records 60 minutes of low-resolution video (640x480) on built-in memory. To dump the video into your computer, simply flip out the camera's built-in USB connector and plug the camera into any USB port on your computer.

The FLIP's built-in microphone will record good sound in quiet places, if you can get close to the source of the sound.

If you want to add an edited sound track to your video, free Total Sound Recorder software turns your computer into a sound recorder and editing station. This allows you to add good quality narration (voice over) and music to your videos.

The camera is so small and lightweight that you really have to make sure you use a tripod or a monopod.

Low-budget HD kit #1

1. Monopod, $19 at local discount store.
2. Targus Grypton portable tripod, $19 at local discount store.
3. Xacti HD1000 HD video camera, $589 from B and H Photo (*www.bhphoto-video.com*).
4. Sony CS10 lavaliere microphone $35, from B and H Photo.
5. Docking station and AC adapter (included with camera).
6. Sandisk Video HD 4GB SDHC memory card, $32.50 from B and H Photo.
7. Remote control for HD1000 camera (included with camera).
8. Operator's manual.

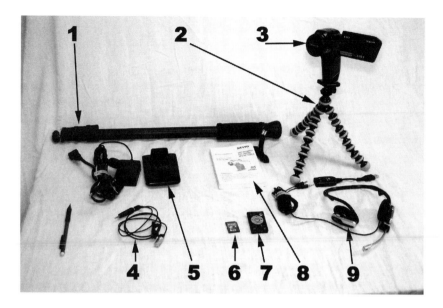

9. Logitech premium Notebook Headset, $60 from Logitech (*www.logitech. com*). (The headset is for listening to audio and for recording narration when you edit.)

10. Camera bag (not shown), $24 at local discount store.

Extra media: 4 GB card.

Lights: None. (Shoot in brightly lit places.)

Computer: Inexpensive Windows laptop, borrowed from a friend.

Editing software: Windows Movie Maker (included with Windows), or any HD editing software that comes with the camera.

Sound recording and editing software: Total Sound Recorder from High Criteria (*www.highcriteria.com*, free download), or any HD editing software that comes with the camera.

Total cost: $778.50.

Comments

You can easily pack this kit in a small camera bag and carry it with you everywhere.

The Xacti camera is easy to use. The HD1000 was an instant hit with journalists. They used it to conduct interviews. It has a microphone jack, so you can connect an external microphone for interviews. Journalists liked the simple controls, on-camera light, high definition output, and ease of operation.

The video quality is HD, and suitable for showing on 50-inch flat screens. To dump the video into your computer, connect a USB cable (supplied with the EX models) between the docking station and a USB connector on your cable.

The camera has a Still Photo feature that takes pretty good stills. The resolution is okay, and the photos are excellent for posting on the web.

With this tiny camera, you need a tripod or monopod for every shot. HD is extremely sensitive to vibration and camera shakes. The slightest movement will show up on the screen. The only time you might shoot without a tripod would be for a situation where you don't particularly care if there is any camera movement.

Most Xacti cameras are bundled with free editing software. My camera came with Ulead MovieFactory. If you decide to buy an Xacti, look around and see what, if any, editing software comes with the camera.

The Xacti is not for everyone. Some people hate the "pistol grip" form factor. Before you commit to an Xacti, try one and make sure you like it.

I like the simplicity, solid-state memory, and convenience of the camera. I can throw my HD1000 in a backpack and be ready to shoot HD wherever I go. With a 4 GB SDHC card in the camera, I can shoot up to 42 minutes of full HD video. I find the camera particularly useful for interviews and data gathering when I am doing research. The HDMI output on the docking station allows me to connect an HDMI cable between the docking station and a flat screen television and immediately watch my footage in HD.

Low-budget HD kit #2

1. Wind screen, "softie windshield" by Rycote (*www.rycote.com*), $110 from B and H Photo (*www.bhphotovideo.com*).
2. Wind screen, foam, for Sennheiser cardioid microphone. $25. (Buy a windscreen to match the model of microphone that you have.)
3. Sennheiser cardioid microphone, $363 at B and H Photo. (Out of production, similar to ME66 but shorter.)
4. XLR adapter, from Beachtek (*www.beachtek.com*), $180 at B and H Photo. (Allows me to use professional microphones on this Sony camera.)

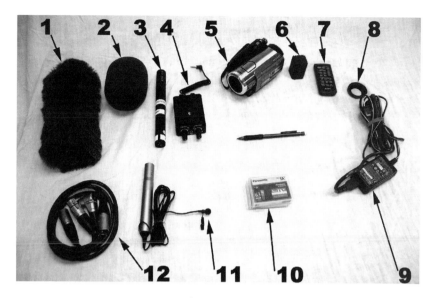

5. Sony HDR-HC7 HDV camera $1,570 on Amazon (*www.amazon.com*).
6. Extra battery, about $60.
7. Remote control for camera (included with camera).
8. 0.55x wide angle lens adapter, 37mm thread, from Century Optics, $120 on Amazon.
9. AC adapter (included with camera).
10.2 Panasonic professional grade DV tapes, $6.
11.Lavaliere microphone, Sony ECM-77B, $395 at B and H Photo.
12.2 microphone cables, 1.5 foot XLR Male to 3-pin XLR Female, $40.
13.Sony MD-7506 Circumaural professional studio headphones, $99 (not shown).
14.Bogen 3246 tripod legs with fluid head, $603 at B and H Photo (not shown).
15.Microphone boom, $20. Bought used from a filmmaker (not shown).
16.Pelican model 1550 hard-shell case $114 at B and H Photo (not shown).

Extra media: Buy DV tapes in bulk at B and H Photo, about $3.50 each.

Lights: Shoot in brightly lit places, and use available light wherever possible. Use reflectors to bounce light into faces. Look into buying an LED light that mounts on the camera.

Computer: I had a Windows computer built specially to edit HDV. It cost me about $1,500.

Editing software: Can be any package that edits HDV. A couple popular ones are Final Cut Pro and Adobe Premiere. Check out Sony Vegas and Pinnacle, too.
Sound recording and editing software: A video editing package that handles HDV will probably have adequate audio editing capability for a low budget production.
Total cost: $3,706, plus $1,500 for the computer.

Comments

This is an expensive kit. Although the camera "only" cost $1,600, the accessories added another $2,100. As a rule of thumb, you won't go far wrong if you figure that the accessories for any camera will cost as much as the camera itself.

The professional microphones were a "one time" expense that added almost $1,000 to the cost of this kit. I rationalized buying these expensive microphones by telling myself that I could use them on my future cameras, too.

The microphones have probably held their value more than anything else I bought. I could probably sell them used for about what I paid new for them a few years ago.

The Sony professional studio headphones have been another excellent buy. When I am in the field, I use them to listen to the audio. They completely cover my ears and I can really hear the sound as recorded. If there is any reverberation, noise, or other problem with the sound, I can hear it instantly. They are also good for listening to Mozart when I get home.

The Bogen tripod has been a workhorse. It was the first expensive tripod I bought, and I still use it.

Soon after I bought the HDR-HC7, the next version of the camera (the HDR-HC9) came out. The HC9 has more features and costs $500 less. (Sigh...) The HC7 was obsolete about the same day I opened the box. This happens more often than not when you buy a camera.

The first thing I do after buying an expensive kit is to buy the best hard-shell camera case that I can afford. I use the case to store and organize the camera, lens adapters, filters, batteries, microphones, cables, operator's manual, and any other accessories that go with a camera. Once I have everything safely tucked away in a case, I know that if I need to shoot some video tomorrow, all I have to do is grab the case, charge the batteries, and go.

High-budget kit

1. Miller DS-5 Solo Carbon Fiber tripod, $1,400 Miller Tripods. American dealer, Markertek (*www.markertek.com*).
2. Batteries for microphone preamplifiers, AA and AAA, $10.
3. AC Adapter and battery charger for camera (included with camera).
4. Tiffen filters, $25 at B and H Photo (*www.bhphotovideo.com*).
5. Hard case from Panasonic, $250.
6. Panasonic DVC 80 DV camera, $2,200.
7. Remote control for camera (included with camera).
8. Extra batteries for camera, $100 at B and H Photo.
9. Panasonic tapes (package of 2), $7 at B and H Photo.
10. Sennheiser shotgun microphone and microphone boom. $40, used from a filmmaker.
11. Sony ECM-77B Lavaliere microphone $395, 2 Sennheiser shotgun microphones, $1,000 from B and H Photo.
12. 3 windshields, 1 Rycote softie $100, 2 Sennheiser foam windscreens $50.
13. 2 microphone cables, 3-pin XLR, $40.

Lights: The first choice is to use available light and shoot in brightly lit places. If you can't shoot in available light, consider buying a lighting kit like the Lowell DV Creator 1 kit, $899.

Computer: I use a Windows machine that cost me $1,500.
Editing software: The popular programs are Adobe Premiere, Apple Final Cut Pro, Sony Vegas, and Avid Express.
Sound recording and editing software: The video editing programs listed have basic audio editing capability.
Total cost: $5,617. Add another $899 for lights if you buy the DV Creator light kit. Add at least $2,500 if you buy a computer and a serious video editing package.

Comments

One thing is missing from this list: an audio field recorder. The field recorder I'd like to add would be a Tascam HD-P2 portable high-definition compact flash stereo field recorder with time code and video sync with an 8 GB microdrive, $1,100 from B and H Photo.

This addition plus a light kit would bring the total kit cost to about $7,600.

The heart of an expensive kit is the camera.

If I were buying a camera today, I would look for an HD camera. I've looked at the Sony, Canon, Panasonic, and JVC cameras—and I liked all of them! They all have stunning image quality. The image tones are slightly different, but not enough to rule out any individual camera.

If I've learned anything about buying cameras, I think it's that I need to know very clearly what I'm buying the camera for before I plunk down my money.

If I were shooting an HD film with a decent budget, I'd look hard at one of the Sony EX series cameras like the Sony PMW-EX1 XDCAM camcorder, $6,449 at B and H Photo. For a day-to-day personal camera I'd probably look at the Canon XH-A1 ($3,299 at B and H Photo), because I like the image quality of the A1.

Some other things you need to know:

- The most popular editing software right now — at least among the people I know — is Apple's Final Cut Pro. Apple seems to have a real commitment to keeping Final Cut Pro updated and abreast of the latest HD changes.

- Define what you want the camera to do. Then talk to people who have used the camera to make the type of film you are considering.
- Look carefully at the camera's workflow. How will you archive, store, and edit the digital output of the camera? (This is a big deal.) What kind of computer will you need? What kind of editing software? Again, talk to someone who has used the camera and has fought all the workflow battles.

Finally, reconsider that however much you spend on the camera, you need to plan to spend an equal amount on the accessories you will need to finish your kit.

Virtual kit

If you are like me, the last thing you want to do is hand the camera work over to someone else, but there are times when doing so makes sense.

Rather than spending your time learning the camera, you might be better off spending your time writing a script, producing a film, or raising money.

What I'm suggesting is that you may be able to assemble a "virtual kit" by hiring professionals. Instead of buying a Sony PMW-EX1 for $6,499 and spending another $5,000 to buy accessories, why not hire a skilled cameraman who already owns the camera? Think of it as hiring the camera with a camera operator attached.

Rates vary, and you can find out the current rates by spending a few afternoons on the telephone. A quick Google search shows me several websites in the San Francisco Bay Area of videographers and camera operators who are looking for work. If you decide to go this route, there's a good chance you may be able to have your production filmed by a professional for less than you would pay to buy a camera.

There are pros and cons to this approach.

Pro: You may get excellent footage.

Pro: You may save money.

Pro: You may finish your film.

Con: If your script stinks or you don't know what you want, you may waste a lot of money. You need to know *exactly* what you want before you hire someone.

Con: Some productions, like documentaries, require a lot of footage. You have to shoot hours, and hours, and hours of stuff before you know exactly what you are looking for. If you're paying by the hour for this, you may quickly go broke and have nothing to show for it.

Con: The camera operator may treat you like an amateur and not listen to anything you say.

Con: You don't get to play with cool cameras.

There are no hard and fast rules for this. Only you know whether you want to hand the work off to professionals. It all depends on how clear you are about what you want, and how skilled you are at working with creative people.

The relationships that people develop while making an independent film can be among the most intense of their lives. The bottom line is that you have to be willing to deal with the inevitable highs and lows of working intimately with a group of passionate people.

If this appeals to you, go for it! You might enjoy it.

CHAPTER 14

YOUTUBE

Several months ago I stepped outside my back door on a beautiful foggy morning. I pressed the record button on my new $149 FLIP camera and panned slowly across my back yard. The result was a 33-second "movie" of my back yard.

I posted the movie on YouTube, just to test the upload process, and promptly forgot about the whole thing.

Recently I went back to YouTube and was amazed to learn that my 33-second movie had 297 views and got a five-star rating!

All I did was hold the camera steady, pan slowly, and make sure I had enough light. If I can get a five-star rating and 297 views by just holding the camera steady and panning slowly, imagine what *you* could do if you really set out to make a movie! This stuff really works.

(The video is here: *http://www.youtube.com/watch?v=Yp744tADZJg*. If this link doesn't work, go to YouTube and search for user *tlevelle* and video title *flip camera test*.)

Now, let's look at how you can create and post your own videos.

What is YouTube?

YouTube is an insanely popular, free online video sharing service. Anyone in the world can upload and watch videos. According to *USA Today*, in 2006 there were over one hundred *million* YouTube views a day!

YouTube is an incredible way for you, as a filmmaker, to get your films out into the world.

How to upload a video to YouTube

1. At your computer, open your browser and go to YouTube (*www.youtube.com*).
2. Click on "Sign Up."
3. When the account details page comes up, enter your personal information including email address, password, user name, and postal code.
4. Click "Create my account." YouTube creates your account.
5. Sign in to your new account.
6. When your account is open, click the "Upload" button on the right side of the page. The Video Upload page opens.

7. Enter a description of your video.
8. Choose a category. (I'm trying to tell people how to use FLIP on YouTube, so I chose "education" from the drop-down menu for Video Category.)
9. Choose tags. (A tag is just a keyword that tells people what is in your video. The keywords — tags — you enter will help people find your video. Be generous when you enter tags. You want people to be able to find your video easily.)
10. Upload. (Click "Upload a video.")

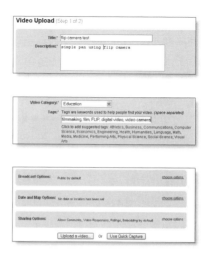

That's all there is to it. You just uploaded your first video to YouTube!

How to create a great YouTube Video

You can increase your chances of creating a great YouTube video by following a few simple rules. The first step is to sure that you submit a video that will look great when YouTube automatically converts your movie into an Adobe Flash video.

Video format

You can upload just about any video format to YouTube. YouTube will automatically convert it to Adobe Flash. Most browsers will play Flash, including Internet Explorer, Firefox, Safari, and Opera.

However, to get a great looking YouTube video, do these things:

1. Follow the YouTube recommendations for format and aspect ratio:
- MPEG4 (DivX, Xvid) format
- 640x480 resolution (720x480 works well, too)
- 64k Mono or 128k Stereo MP3 audio
- 30 FPS (frames per second)
- Aspect ratio of 4:3 (most standard definition DV cameras)

2. Use a high-quality video editing program like Windows Movie Maker, Adobe Premiere, Apple iMovie, Apple Final Cut Pro, or Sony Vegas. Some editing

programs now have settings that allow you to output the ideal YouTube format with one click.

3. Keep your movie about two minutes long or less.

4. Start your show immediately. Don't have long credits or titles before the show begins. If you really want to put titles on the movie, make a very short title — five to ten seconds. Put everything else, like your name and your website, at the end of the video.

5. Show the situation or the premise of your video in the first few seconds.

Camera

Use a camera that shoots 640x480 (like the FLIP) or 720x480 (most DV cameras).

Use 4x3 aspect ratio, and not 16x9.

Use the four basic shots: establishing shot, long shot, medium shot, close-up.

Use a tripod if possible.

Use pans and tilts.

Move the camera sloooowly.

Lighting

Shoot where you have plenty of light — but not too little and not too much.

Don't point the camera into the sun.

Sound

If your camera has an AGC (audio Automatic Gain Control) switch, turn it ON. If your camera does not have an AGC switch, don't worry about it. (Later, you may want to turn off AGC and experiment with sound, but to get started, leave AGC ON.)

If your camera has a microphone jack, use an external microphone for interviews and audio recording. The closer the microphone is to the source of the sound, the better your sound will be.

Story

A good story is the most important part of making a good video. It's also the hardest. Every successful video, whether fiction or nonfiction, tells a good story. Professional filmmakers spend years learning how to tell stories, and it is an interesting study. But you and I don't have years. You want to have fun and make a neat video right now.

Here are a few tips that I've picked up after years of judging film festival entries, and writing about how to tell stories in my co-authored book, *Producing with Passion*.

1. In general, keep your first videos well under five minutes. It gets very hard to hold an audience once you've gone over five minutes. At about five minutes you will lose the audience if you don't have a good story.
2. Start the story quickly. You only have a few seconds at the beginning of the video to capture people's attention. Don't waste them.
3. Have a compelling central character. Advertisers know this — that's why they use striking, attractive people in their commercials. Your central character need not be beautiful, but he or she must be *interesting*!
4. Tell a story about something that is personally important to you. Not something that is important to someone you want to impress, but something that really matters to you.

If you do these four things, you will have a very good chance of making a video that people will want to watch.

Good luck, and good storytelling!

Online YouTube resources

YouTube Online Handbook
The handbook is at *www.youtube.com/t/yt_handbook_produce*

Putting YouTube videos on your website
You can find all the information you need here: *http://www.youtube.com/youtubeonyoursite*

Watching YouTube videos on your phone
This tells you how to watch YouTube videos on your cell phone: *www.youtube.com/mobile*

Streaming YouTube video directly from your webcam
A YouTube video can come directly from your webcam. To learn how to do this, go to *www.youtube.com/t/explore_youtube* and click on the Quick Capture button.

CHAPTER 15

DO'S AND DON'TS

H ere is a quick list of illustrated "do's and don'ts" that covers the essentials of *Digital Video Secrets*. (You can find expanded discussions of all these topics in the earlier chapters of Digital Video Secrets.)

Getting started

As the old saying goes, "Well begun is half done."

Do make sure you have everything you need before you start

Before you leave home, take a moment to make sure you have everything you need.

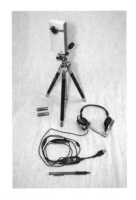

Do shoot a short test before you start

Shoot some test footage and make sure everything works. Play the test back on a computer monitor or TV. Check both picture and sound.

Don't grab the camera and run out the door

Many problems result from hasty and poorly prepared departures.

Don't shoot in restricted locations

Do NOT shoot in restricted locations. Many locations are now restricted. If in doubt, check it out! You don't want to have your camera confiscated or worse, be arrested.

Shooting fluently and confidently

When you learn to shoot fluently and confidently, your images will improve dramatically.

Do get comfortable with your camera.

The best way to become comfortable with your camera is to turn it on and play with it. Push all the buttons. Learn to use every control on the camera.

Do put your movies online

Online video sites like YouTube are a great way to get your videos seen and appreciated. The YouTube chapter tells you how to do this.

YouTube accounts are free at *www.youtube. com*.

Do learn to "see" with the camera

One of the keys to getting good images is to learn to "see" with the camera. Practice "seeing" the world through the LCD or view-finder of your camera.

Do learn to shoot intuitively

Go for a walk with your camcorder. When you see something that interests you, stop and shoot 30 seconds of footage. Don't worry about sound, light, story — or anything technical. Just shoot.

Do learn to shoot "from the hip"

One day, you are going to have to shoot "from the hip." Practice now so you will be prepared. Use the viewfinder or LCD to frame a scene. Adjust the camcorder's zoom, focus, shutter, iris, and white balance. Then close the LCD and hold the camera at waist level. Point the camera toward the scene and press "Record."

Do learn to shoot with both eyes open

With one eye on the viewfinder and the other eye open, walk about a location as you record video. Don't lower the camcorder until you shoot at least five minutes of footage.

Composing powerful, compelling images

Do use the four basic shots

For every scene you shoot, try to get four basic shots: Establishing Shot, Long Shot, Medium Shot and Close Up.

Establishing shot (ES)

Long shot (LS)

Medium shots (MS)

Close-ups (CU)

Do use the five basic camera angles

Use the basic five angles when you shoot: looking down, looking up, straight on, Dutch angle, and angle plus angle.

Looking-down: The camera is above a person and looking down on him or her.

Looking-up: The camera is below a person and looking up to him or her.

Straight-on: The camera is looking straight on at the person.

Dutch angle: A "Dutch angle" means that you simply tilt the camera right or left.

Angle plus angle : When you combine two angles (up and left, for example) you have what is called an "angle plus angle" shot.

Do use both objective and subjective views
Objective view
The camera shows what the audience would see if they were standing off to one side of the scene and watching.

Subjective view
The camera shows what a character in the scene would see.

Do compose on the rule of thirds
Mentally divide the screen in thirds and place important visual elements on these lines.

Do look for ways to add perspective
Common ways of adding perspective in films: train tracks and roads that recede in the distance.

Do look for diagonal lines
Look for diagonal lines in your shots. Compose your image so the diagonal lines draw the viewer's eye to important elements of the picture.

Do look for triangles

Create a visual triangle by framing your shot so that three dominant elements in a scene are at the points of an imaginary triangle. The audience will subconsciously "create" a story from the three elements.

Do create images which have "layers" of meaning

One of the most powerful techniques you can use to create compelling images is a "layered" image with three elements in spatial relationship to each other.

For example, the front "layer" of your image may be one character. Behind this character is a second character looking at the first, and behind these two characters is a third character looking at the other two.

Supporting and moving your camera

How you support and move the camera affects your video profoundly. For example, rock-solid, tripod-mounted shots and smooth, even moves may give a feeling of stability. Jerky, abrupt hand-held shots may give a feeling of breathlessness.

Do use a tripod

The standard advice for buying a tripod is "Get the best tripod you can afford." Think of your tripod as an investment in your shooting career.

Do use tilts

To do a "tilt," simply move the camera slowly up or slowly down. In a tilt-down, you start at the sky and slowly tilt down. A tilt-up starts at the ground and slowly moves up.

Move the camera very slowly, much more slowly than you first imagine.

Do use pans

A pan is a sideways movement of the camera. The trick to doing a good pan is to move the camera slowly. If you pan the camera to follow a person, keep the person's image in the center of the frame.

Do learn how to shoot hand-held

The trick to shooting hand-held is to keep the camera steady. Brace yourself against a wall or other support. Use OIS (Optical Image Support) if your camera has this function. Move the camera slowly, and practice, practice, practice.

In the picture, Barbara is:
1) Using both hands to hold the camera steady and
2) Braced against the wall.

Don't shoot bad hand-held footage

Don't move the camera quickly, or allow the camera to jiggle. If you do, you may end up with shaky "jiggle cam" footage.

Lighting

Non-professional shooters may keep on shooting badly lit shots for years because they don't have a system to analyze and correct lighting problems.

The four major problems with lighting for digital video are:
- Too little light
- Too much light
- Lighting has the wrong ratio, direction or color
- White balance problems

Don't shoot with too little light

When you don't have enough light, your images may be "muddy," colorless, and noisy (white speckles in the image).

Ways to cope with low light:
- Add light.
- Increase video gain.
- Open the iris (increase the aperture by choosing a lower f-stop).
- Lower the shutter speed.
- Shoot at a different time of day, or in a different location.

Don't shoot with too much light

When you have too much light, the highlights in your images will be "blown out" (white areas with no detail).

- Adjust your camera exposure using zebra stripes; if your camera has zebra stripes, turn them on. Diagonal lines will appear in the viewfinder every place where the image is over-exposed. Close the iris — increase the F-stop — until the zebra stripes barely disappear. When the stripes barely disappear, you can shoot safely.
- Use an ND (neutral density) filter to reduce amount of light reaching the sensor.
- Increase the shutter speed.
- Shoot at a different time of day, or in a different location.

Do set white balance

When your image has a weird tint — usually blue, green or yellow — you probably need to set the camera's white balance. Read your camera manual for instructions on how to do this.

Do use the "big light in the sky" (the sun) wisely

At sunrise, the sun gives a nice soft golden light. As noon approaches, the light gets "harder" and quite bluish. Toward sunset, the light gets "softer" and golden again. If you shoot during mid-day, you will have a hard, bluish light.

Do bounce the light

Use a reflector to "bounce" some soft, gentle light back into people's faces.

Do mix natural and artificial light

If your scene is lit by a combination of natural and artificial light, set the white balance of the camera in the mixed light. Place your white card next to the subject and white balance the camera on the white card.

Shooting footage that you can edit

You need more than pretty pictures when you shoot, you need shots that you can edit into a compelling movie.

Do make a shot list before you shoot

The apparently simple act of making a shot list draws upon all the elements of filmmaking:

1. Knowing your subject intimately.
2. Knowing what story you are telling.
3. Visualizing your movie.

Do get the essential images

Before you shoot, go through your shot list and identify the "must-have" shots. Get these shots, no matter what else happens.

Shots to consider:

- Establishing shot of the location.
- Master shot of the activity or scene (a wide shot that shows the entire scene).
- Medium shots of the essential activities.

- Close-ups of essential people.
- "Once in a lifetime" shots (the bride and groom's first kiss, a marathon runner crossing the finish line, the only interview with a celebrity).

Do shoot sequences

Everything happens in sequences, whether it's cooking a meal, driving a car, or meeting someone for lunch. Always look for the sequences in what you shoot. Try to film the key images in an activity — from beginning to end.

Do get reaction shots

Reaction shots are close-ups of people's emotional reactions. Candid reaction shots give the final video increased emotional power and intimacy.

Do shoot cutaways

A cutaway is a picture of something in the environment that you can "cut" to when editing the scene.

A close-up of the interviewee's hands as he or she twists the watch would be a motivated cutaway, because it gives a hint of the interviewee's mental state.

Close-ups of animals almost always work as cutaways, for some reason.

Do have a low shooting ratio

Your "shooting ratio" is the amount of footage you shoot compared to the amount of footage in your final film. If you shoot twenty minutes of video to make a one-minute film, your shooting ratio is 20:1.

Sometimes you can't keep a low shooting ratio. When you are shooting a documentary, you may not have any choice except to shoot *lots* of footage in hopes of getting the few moments that you need to tell your story.

The higher the shooting ratio, the longer it is going to take you to finish your film. For one thing, you have to log all the footage and make decisions on how to use it.

Do label your media

Label your tapes and other media with:
1. Date
2. Name of shot or scene
3. Your name
4. Your phone number

Do slate your shots

Slating is the practice of taking a five-second picture of a whiteboard or slate at the beginning of each shot. It is an "on camera" label at the beginning of each shot.

The slate should include:
1. Date
2. Time
3. Name of shot or scene
4. "Take" number (if you are doing multiple takes)
5. Your name

Getting good sound

Sound is important, really important.

Sound is one of the two most likely things that will mess you up. (The other thing that will mess you up is story.)

Sound recording is at least as difficult as cinematography. A good sound person will spend years mastering the craft. A dedicated sound person may cheap when you compare the cost to the total expense of your film or production.

Do consider hiring a professional sound person

Things to look for in a sound professional:
1. Experience working on films or productions like yours.
2. A good portfolio of soundtracks.
3. A willingness to work on independent, low-budget productions.
4. A desire to work on *your* production.

Don't try to "fix the sound in postproduction"

Fixing sound in postproduction is usually time consuming and difficult. Sometimes it's impossible. (In Hollywood sound *is* done in postproduction, but then they spend millions of dollars on a picture.)

Do scout all your locations for sound

The two main problems with location sound are noise and reverberation. Record some sound in the exact spots where you intend to shoot. Play the recording back later and listen for potential problems.

Do know how to use the on-camera mike for interviews

Normally, you never want to use the on-camera mike for interviews. However, if you have no other choice but to use the on-camera microphone for interviews, here's how to do it:

- Do the interview in a quiet place.
- Open the lens wide (zoom out) and get the camera as close to the speaker as possible.

Do listen to the sound when you are shooting

When you are in the field, someone should listen to all the sound as it is recorded. If you are running a "one man band," this person will be you.

The best way to listen is with a good pair of studio headphones.

Do use directional microphones

A directional microphone will pick up good dialog from up to a couple feet away. The pickup patterns of directional microphones vary. Experiment with different microphones until you find the one with a sound that appeals to you.

Do use a boom

A good way to use a directional microphone is to attach it to a boom. Use the boom to hold the microphone overhead, with the microphone pointing down at the speaker.

Do mount a directional microphone on your camera

Some prosumer cameras come with special mounts for directional microphones. The microphone is usually mounted above the camera in a rubberized holder.

Do use windscreens on your microphones

The slightest breeze or movement of air can cause wind noise as the air moves over a microphone. You should assume that you need a wind screen all the time, on every microphone.

The directional microphone in this picture has a nice soft Rycote Softie windscreen.

Do use lavaliere microphones for dialog

Lavaliere microphones are tiny microphones that you clip to clothing, usually within eight inches or so of the interviewee's lips.

GLOSSARY

Adams, Ansel: famous US photographer and inventor of the Zone system.

ADR (automated dialog replacement): the process of adding dialogue to a movie after photography is complete.

AE (automatic exposure): a control that tells the camera to calculate the best exposure automatically.

AE Shift: a control that sets the automatic exposure higher or lower than normal.

AGC (automatic gain control): camera function that controls its sound recording levels. Useful in noisy situations, or situations where you might have sudden loud sounds, like a busy street. AGC is less useful in quiet situations, like an interview in a quiet room.

Ambient sound: the background sound in any location.

Angle (camera): the position of the camera in relation to the activity being filmed.

Aperture: the size of the opening in the camera lens, measured in "f- stops". A smaller f -stop is a larger aperture. Larger apertures allow filming in less light but decrease the depth of field. Smaller apertures allow filming in more light, but increase the depth of field.

Artificial (light): light coming from an artificial source like a lamp.

Assemble (edit): a preliminary edit that shows the general outline of your movie. Useful as a fast way to find out if your show "works" and as a way to find out what scenes you should add or delete.

Audio gain: an adjustment that controls how much the audio signal is amplified.

Auto exposure: the mode in which the camera chooses the aperture and shutter speed automatically. Auto exposure can be very useful, because modern cameras are quite good at choosing the proper exposure.

Auto focus: the mode in which the camera focuses for you. Most cameras will automatically focus on whatever is in the middle of the frame. The common problem with autofocus is hunting, in which the camera often loses focus and moves the lens back and forth trying to require focus. In manual focus, the camera lens is focused on one point and stays there.

Auto mode: sometimes called full auto. The camera does everything: focus, white balance, sound gain, video gain. Use only when you have no other choice, for example you have to shoot something *right now* and don't have time to set all the controls manually.

Automatic gain control. *See* AGC.

Available (light): the light normally available in a setting.

Backlit: light coming from behind the subject. For example, when the sun is behind your subject and you are shooting into the sun, your subject is backlit. In general, avoid backlit subjects unless you are shooting into the sun for effect.

Black: an advanced video setting that changes the dynamic area within the black areas of a video image. Black stretch increases the dynamic range within a black area. Black press reduces the dynamic range in a black area. *See* Secret 68.

Blown highlights: when the highlights in a scene are overexposed. When a highlight is blown, it is completely white and there is no detail in the white.

Boom: a long pole used to hold a microphone over a person who is speaking. The microphone is usually held close enough to get good sound, but far enough away that it doesn't show on the video.

Bounce: using a reflector to bounce light onto a scene, as in "bounce some light onto the scene." Usually used as a way to get additional light onto an actor's face.

Cameraman: the person operating the camera. When the cameraman is responsible for lighting as well is operating camera, he or she is known as the lighting cameraman.

CD (compact disc): the standard for distributing audio for home entertainment.

Chrominance: the part of the video signal that carries color information.

Close-up: an image in which the subject is very close to the camera.

Color Matrix: advanced video setting. The color matrix determines how a camera generates colors. *See* Secret 72.

Colorbar chart: a chart with standard colors printed on it. These specific colors generate a known video signal on a vector scope and waveform monitor.

Composing (an image): arranging the visual elements of a scene to evoke a specific emotional response in an audience.

Consumer microphone: inexpensive, low-quality microphones designed for consumer cameras and consumer audio gear.

Crew: the people that work behind the camera. A crew may be one person (you) or it may be dozens of people. The minimum crew is generally two people: one person for camera and one person for sound.

Cutaways: images of secondary things or people in the environment in which a video is being shot. Cutaways are necessary for smooth editing. More cutaways are better than fewer. Go for a ratio of one minute of cutaways for every three minutes of interviews or primary footage.

Cuts: the transition point between different chunks of footage. The word "cut" comes from film editing. In the early days of moviemaking, the editor would physically cut the strip of film at the end of the scene and then splice it to the next chunk.

Dialog: what people say— the spoken words.

Diopter adjustment: an adjustment on the viewfinder of a digital video camera that matches the optics of the viewfinder to the vision of the user. Usually it's a small lever under the viewfinder. While looking through the viewfinder, move the lever until the image is in focus. The diopter adjustment only changes the viewfinder; it does not focus the lens.

Directional microphone: a microphone that is designed to pick up more sound from a certain direction than from other directions. A directional microphone still has to be located as close to the source of sound as possible; it just doesn't have to be as close as other microphones.

Documentarian: a person who makes documentary films.

Documentary (film): a film that documents the real world, and real people.

Dolly: a wheeled cart used to move the camera (and cameraman). You can rent a commercial dolly from a movie equipment rental house. However, over the years students and independent filmmakers have used just about everything imaginable for a dolly: shopping carts, hand trucks, skate boards, and little red wagons.

Dump (footage into your computer): the process of getting your video into your computer. As in, "Dump it into the computer and let's see what we have."

DV (digital video): the acronym DV can mean several things. The most common usages are 1) digital video, and 2) an industry standard for cameras and other recording devices.

DVD (digital video disc): the standard for distributing movies for home entertainment.

Edit (assemble): an "assemble edit" is the first pass at editing a video. You don't worry about anything in the footage except pasting together what you have. It's a way to see what you have and what you might still need.

Edit (in camera): an "in-camera edit" is a way of shooting a video so that all the shots are in a sequence. You plan each shot before you shoot it. When you are done shooting, your show is done, without any other editing (a very useful skill to have).

Editing program, sound: a "sound editing program" is a program designed for editing audio. It has specialized features to get the best out of the audio that you record with your show. Cakewalk (*www.cakewalk.com*) is a popular manufacturer of audio hardware and software.

Editing program, video: a "video editing program" is a program designed for editing video. Most computers come with some sort of basic video editing program built in to the operating system. There are many video editing programs. Popular ones include: Final Cut from Apple (*www.apple.com*) and Premiere from Adobe (*www.adobe.com*).

Establishing shot: a wide-angle shot of the location or setting for your video. The "establishing shot" tells the viewer where the action is taking place.

Event videographer: someone who makes a living taking videos of events.

Event: any scheduled activity. For example, a wedding, football game, political rally and a family reunion are all "events."

Field recorder. *See* recorder, field.

Film festival: a place where filmmakers gather to show their work. A film festival is the main avenue for many filmmakers to display their work to film critics, production companies, media, and other filmmakers. Large film companies like Miramax send buyers to major film festivals in search of new films to distribute. *Withoutabox.com* is a website that lists film festivals worldwide.

Film look: making video images look like film images.

Film student: a person studying filmmaking.

Filmmaker, independent: a person who is making a film without the backing of a major studio.

Flip camera: a small, simple camera marketed by FLIP (*www.theflip.com*). The FLIP camera is a simple, low cost way to shoot video for video sharing sites like YouTube. The FLIP has solid-state memory (no tapes). A USB connector flips out (hence the name) and you plug the camera into the USB connector of your computer to transfer the video to the computer.

Fluorescent: a white-balance setting on your camera that compensates for the greenish light of many fluorescent light bulbs. Different brands and types of fluorescent bulbs have a wide variety of light colors.

Focus assist: a function on HD cameras that helps you focus the camera accurately.

Focus chart: a chart that shows you when your camera is in focus. Often used in professional productions where each shot must be of maximum quality.

Footage: the recorded images from a video camera, for example, "We got good footage of the wedding."

Frame rate: the number of times (rate) per second that a video camera fills the screen with a picture. In North America, this rate is 30. In Europe and Asia it is 25. In movie theaters, the rate is 24.

Frame: one full screen of an image. The number of images per second is the frame rate. Video can be recorded at different frame rates.

F-stop: a way of measuring the size of the opening (aperture) in a lens. The higher the f-stop, the smaller the opening.

Full auto mode: the mode in which the camera does everything. Useful if you have to pick up the camera and shoot immediately. Generally, however, you want to avoid full auto. In full auto, the camera often focuses on the wrong things, sets a white balance wrong, and sets the sound gain (AGC) wrong. You should only use full auto when the subject is so compelling that the audience forgives you for the awful picture.

Gel: thin sheets of plastic used to reduce or change the color of the light passing through them. Color correction gels change the light's color. ND (neutral density) gels reduce the light without changing its color.

Grayscale chart: a chart with a standard series of gray tones from very light to very dark.

Hand-held: a method of shooting in which you hold the camera in your hand, and do not use a tripod. The ability to shoot hand-held is very useful, but it is very difficult to do well.

HD (high definition): high-resolution video suitable for large flat screen televisions. There is no one common standard HD, but the goal that many people seem to be aiming for is 30 progressive frames, of 1080 lines.

HDV: an inexpensive high-definition video format.

Headphone effect: a "hiss" often heard in headphones. Caused by the closeness of the headphones to the ear. The hiss may not be noticeable when you listen to the sound on regular speakers.

Highlights: brightest part of an image.

In the mud: when sound is too low and you can't separate it from the background noise, it is said to be "in the mud." This problem is not fixable.

Independent film: a film made by an independent filmmaker, or an independent film company. These days an independent film can mean anything from a $5,000 film made by the kid down the street to a multi-million dollar production with a crew of hundreds of people.

Independent filmmaker: a person who makes an independent film.

Interview footage: a recording of an interview. Interview footage is often used heavily in documentaries.

Jib: a long pole with a camera on one end and a counterbalance on the other end.

Jiggle cam: a derogatory term for shaky hand-held footage. Also known as "vomit cam" for the nausea-inducing effect of watching such footage.

Jumps: abrupt change in camera angle, location, or setting between two chunks of footage.

Labeling: writing the topic, date, and your name on every tape you shoot.

Lavaliere microphone: a small microphone designed to be clipped to an interviewee's clothing. Best placed within six to nine inches of the interviewee's mouth.

LCD (liquid crystal display): the flip out display on the side of most video cameras is commonly called "the LCD."

Lighting ratio: the difference in amount of light falling on someone's face, or on a scene. A commonly used lighting ratio for faces is 4:1, or two f-stops from brightest to darkest.

Location: a place where video is shot.

Long shot: a shot that shows most of a subject's body. It is taken from "a long way away," thus the term "long shot."

Low light: a setting or condition where you have very little light. For example, "It was a low light shoot," or "How does the camera perform under low light conditions?"

Low-budget film: a film made with little money. The term has become almost meaningless because it can mean anything from a $5,000 film made by an unknown film student to a multi-million dollar film with major Hollywood talent.

Manual focus: the practice of focusing a camera manually.

Manual mode: the mode in which you manually set focus, exposure, and white balance. You adjust the camera to match the situation in which you are shooting. Use manual mode to get the best possible image from your camera.

Master shot: an overall shot of a scene. When shooting video, it can be one continuous shot — from a second camera — from start to finish of a scene, interview, or activity. The master shot is very useful when it comes time to edit your footage.

Media: what the video signal is recorded upon. Media used to be one thing — videotape. These days the digital video signal can be recorded on anything that will record digital information including videotape cassettes, hard drive, flash drive, solid-state memory or optical disk recorder — a recorder that uses optical disks to record video. Some camcorders record on optical disks.

Medium shot: a shot that shows the head and shoulders of a person. It is "medium close" to the person.

Mike: short for microphone.

Mini-jack: small audio connector. Mostly used on inexpensive cameras, micro-phones, and audio equipment.

Natural light: light coming from the sun.

ND (neutral density) filter: a glass or plastic filter that reduces the amount light passing through it without changing the color of the light. ND filters are built in to many camcorders. Use the ND filter when filming in very bright light, for example in full sunlight.

Netflix: a company that rents DVDs of movies. They recently started online rentals as well. Netflix is very useful for filmmakers. Their website is *www.netflix.com*.

Noise: the background noise in an audio or video signal. In audio noise can be anything from a crackling sound, to a hiss, to a rumble. In video, noise shows up as white "speckles" and "grain" in the image.

NTSC: the analog television standard in North America and a few other places. The acronym NTSC officially stands for National Television System Committee. After watching their shows being shown on different television screens, some filmmakers claim that NTSC really means "Never The Same Color twice."

Numbers game: destructive mental trap in which a filmmaker starts comparing camera "numbers" (specifications) endlessly.

OIS (optical image stabilization): a way of stabilizing an image within a digital video camera. OIS systems have improved dramatically in the past few years. Some filmmakers claim that with OIS they can shoot hand-held footage that looks like it was shot using a tripod. It is important to remember that good hand-held shooting takes practice, whether you use OIS or not.

On-camera microphone: the built-in microphone that comes with the camera. Usually, the on-camera microphone is a poor choice for recording voices or sounds. In most cases the microphone is not close enough to the source of the sound, and the quality of the microphone is relatively poor.

PAL: an analog broadcast television standard used in Europe, Asia and parts of Africa. PAL is an acronym for Phase Alternating Line.

Pan: the practice of moving the camera from right to left. Often used to follow an actor as he or she walks through a scene. For example, "Let's pan left and follow Jane as she walks through the door and across the room."

Post: short for postproduction. Postproduction is everything that happens to a movie after the images are recorded. Typical postproduction tasks include editing, color correction, editing and laying in sound tracks, music, narration and titles.

Production effects: an audio recording of the overall sound at a particular location. On small productions the on-camera microphone may be used to record production effects, while another microphone is used to record voices and dialog. The production effects recording may include things like traffic on a freeway, trucks pulling into a driveway, footsteps on gravel, birds chirping in the trees, or waves crashing on a nearby shore.

Prosumer: a combination of the words "professional" and "consumer." A prosumer camera has fewer features than a professional camera but more than a consumer camera. Prosumer cameras are so powerful these days that they may be used in "professional" applications like news gathering and independent filmmaking.

Push-to-focus: a button on some cameras that allows you to momentarily engage the auto focus features of the camera. Useful when you need to focus quickly and accurately.

Reaction shot: a shot that shows a person's instinctive emotional reaction to something that just happened onscreen.

Reframe (the image): moving the camera and re-composing the image.

Reverberation: reflected sound that bounces back and forth in a room or location, for example within a gymnasium or a room with hard walls. Reverberation on a sound recording cannot be fixed.

Scout (locations): the act of visiting a location before shooting begins, as in "I'll go scout the location tomorrow." Locations should be scouted for both sound (noise and reverberation) and visuals (lighting, background images).

Scratch track: a throw-away sound track used for synchronizing sound and picture. Often, the on-camera microphone of a camcorder is used to record a scratch track, while a second, better microphone is used to record the actual dialog. *See also* Production Effects.

Screen ratio: the ratio between the height and width of the video screen. SD screens (older televisions) are 4:3. HD screens (newer televisions) are generally 16:9.

SD (standard definition): the standard for analog broadcast television signals for the past fifty years. Standard definition video is rapidly becoming obsolete. It is being replaced by HD (high definition) video. By law all TV broadcast switched to digital in February 2009. Users of SD require an adapter box to view on-air films.

Sequences: the steps in which things happen, for example, opening the door, walking in the house, sitting down.

Shoot: to record something using a film or video camera, for example, "We borrowed Sally's video camera to shoot the wedding."

Shooting ratio: the ratio between the amount of footage you shoot and the final show. For example, if you shoot twenty hours of footage and edit it down to one hour, your shooting ratio would be 20:1.

Shot list: a list of shots that you intend to take at a certain location.

Shotgun microphone: a long, slender directional microphone.

Shots: individual recordings. Generally the time between START and STOP recording.

Shutter speed: how long the image sensor is exposed to light, for example 1/3 second is a "slow shutter speed," 1/60 second is "normal," and 1/1000 is a "fast shutter speed."

Shutter: the device that controls how long the image sensor is exposed to an image. Times are measured in fractions of a second. These times are called shutter speeds. Slower shutter speeds give a slightly blurred image, while higher shutter speeds appear to freeze motion.

Slate: a whiteboard or piece of paper with shot information written on it. The slate is the first thing recorded. It tells the editor what the shot is. In early Hollywood, the "slate" was a piece of slate upon which the information would be written in chalk.

Slating: the act of shooting a slate at the beginning of a shot or scene.

Sound person: the one person on location who is paying attention to sound.

Sound track: the audio part of a video production.

Star chart: a type of focus chart. It has a star pattern that seems to "pop" into focus when the lens is focused properly.

Sun: the "big light" in the sky. The source of all natural light. Reflectors may be used to fill in the harsh shadows that often occur when using bright sunlight.

Test chart: a chart containing the precise colors required to generate a specific video signal. Sometimes called a test card. One of the largest manufacturers of video test charts is DSC (*www.dsc.com*).

Theatrical release: distributing, or releasing, a film to show it in theaters.

Three-point lighting: standard lighting technique in which the subject is lit from three directions by three lights. The three lights are called the key light, back light, and fill light.

Tilt: shooting technique in which the camera is slowly tilted up or down while recording. A tilt-up usually starts at the ground and goes up. A tilt-down usually starts at the sky and goes down.

Toy camera: an inexpensive or free camera. Usually has low resolution and poor sound recording capability.

Tripod: the best way to support your camera. The tripod legs are sometimes called "sticks."

Trust: what you need if you are going to interview someone.

Unifying theme: a theme that links different images, for example a grape vineyard, a cluster of grapes, and a farm worker pruning a grape vine.

Urban grit: a shooting style. In this style the camera moves all the time, and pans quickly between speakers. Popular on "edgy" movies and TV shows that are set in an urban area.

UV filter: a clear glass filter that goes on the front of your camera lens. Some people use UV filters to protect the camera lens.

Vector scope: a scope that displays the video signal so you can analyze it. Most advanced editing programs have vector scopes built in. You need a recording of a test chart to make the best use of a vector scope.

Verite: a style of camera work in which the camera operator acts as a neutral observer and recorder of reality. Verite camera operators strive to be as invisible as a "fly on the wall."

Video editing software: software that allows you to edit video on your computer. There are many editing programs; some of the most well-known are Vegas, Adobe Premiere, and Apple iMovie and Apple Final Cut Pro.

Video gain: an adjustment that controls how much the video signal is amplified.

Vomit cam. *See* jiggle cam.

Waveform monitor: a scope that displays certain elements of a video signal. Most advanced editing programs have waveform monitors built in. You need a recording of a test chart to make the best use of a waveform monitor.

Weddings: hopeful events that often require the services of event videographers.

White balance: the process of telling the camera what to use as a reference point for generating video colors. Video cameras have no idea what the color in a scene should be. The only way a camera knows what the colors should be is by knowing first what pure white is. When you tell the camera something is white, it uses that thing to generate the rest of the colors.

White card: a card that is printed with a precise shade of white. Used as a reference to "white balance" a video camera.

Wind screen: a microphone cover that reduces the noise that wind makes when it blows across a microphone. Sensitive microphones can even pick up wind noise from the movement of air within a building. Wind noise sometimes sounds like a "rumble" that drowns out all other sound.

Wired microphone: a microphone that is connected to the recorder or camcorder by a wire.

Wireless microphone: a microphone that is connected to the recorder or camcorder by a wireless transmitter and receiver.

XLR jack: three-pin audio connector found on commercial grade audio equipment and some high-end camcorders.

Zebra stripes: some cameras have a feature in which stripes show up in the viewfinder to indicate overexposed areas in a scene. Zebra stripes only show up in the viewfinder, and are not recorded on the image itself. A very useful way to find out which areas of your image might be over exposed before you start recording.

Zone system: a system of understanding and setting exposure. The system was invented by the American photographer Ansel Adams.

Zoom: making the image in a lens appear larger by adjusting the focal length of an adjustable lens. Beginners often over-use zoom. When recording, the general rule is "fingers off the zoom."

A P P E N D I X

DIGITAL VIDEO CAMERA WORKSHEET

Make copies and use them as a way to organize the information you gather about cameras.

Camera Name and model _____

Price: _____ Vendor: _____

Is the price within your budget: Y / N _____

How much more will accessories cost? _____

(See accessory worksheet)

Camera tryout checklist

1. Operate the camera. What is important is how it feels to *you*.

Operated it? Y / N _____

Feel right? Y / N _____

Size OK? _____ Y / N _____

Controls OK? Y / N_____

2. View the image on a good monitor or large screen TV. Note your impressions. What is important is how it looks to *you*.

Like image? Y / N _____

Colors good? Y / N_____

Resolution good? Y / N_____

3. No camera is perfect.

What bugs you about this one?_____

Can you live with it? Y/ N _____

Camera technical info worksheet

Sensor:

      size _____ type _____ mega pixels _____ 16x9? _____

Lens

      Range (f-stop)   _____ - _____

      Range (mm)   _____ - _____

      Filter size (mm) _____

Optical zoom amount _____

Optical Image Stabilizer Y / N

Lux (minimum) _____

Recording System   NTSC / PAL /Other

Recording Format   _____

Audio range _____ HZ - _____ HZ

Time Code Y / N

Date & Time Y / N

A/V Dubbing Y / N

Viewfinder:

Color / BW   Pixels _____

LCD Monitor

      Size _____

      Widescreen 16:9 Y / N

      Swivels?   Y / N

Manual Controls

      Zoom   Y / N

      White Balance   Y / N

      Shutter Speed   Y / N

      Iris   Y / N

      Focus   Y / N

      Mic Level   Y / N

      Other   _____

      Other   _____

Other   _____

Other   _____

Built-in Light   Y / N

Built-in Mic   Y / N

Built-in Speaker   Y / N

Accessory Shoe   Y / N

Media (for video recording)

Tape _____   Tape Loading   Top/Bottom/Side

Flash memory _____   Type _____ Size _____

Hard Disk _____   Size _____

DVD   Type _____ Size _____

Card Slot (for stills or scene settings) Y/N

Type _____ Size _____

Input/Output Connectors

Line In Recording Y/N

Inputs

I-Link ®   Y / N   How many? _____

1394 (FireWire)   Y / N   How many? _____

Other _____

Other _____

Outputs

I-Link ®   Y / N   How many? _____

1394 (FireWire)   Y / N   How many? _____

Multi A/V   Y / N   How many? _____

USB   Y / N   How many? _____

Component video   Y / N   How many? _____

S-Video   Y / N   How many? _____

HDMI   Y / N   How many? _____

Other _____

Other _____

Other _____

Microphone Input   Y / N   Type? _____ How many? __

Headphone Jack   Y / N

DIGITAL VIDEO ACCESSORY WORKSHEET

Accessories can cost as much or more than the camera.

Sound Checklist

1. What external microphones will you need?

    Type   Cost

    _____   _____

    _____   _____

    _____   _____

2. Wind screen(s) for the microphones

    Type   Cost

    _____   _____

    _____   _____

    _____   _____

3. Do you need a boom?

    Type   Cost

    _____   _____

4. Do you need a mixer?

    Type   Cost

    _____   _____

5. Cables

    Type   Cost

    _____   _____

6. Other?

    Type   Cost

    _____   _____

    _____   _____

Tripod

    Type   Cost

    _____   _____

Lighting Checklist

If you plan to shoot available light, shoot some tests to verify that available light gives you the image you need.

You may decide to consider a basic DV lighting kit.

Lighting kit Y/N   Cost _____
Bounce reflectors Y/N   Cost _____
_____   Cost _____
_____   Cost _____

Basic Camera Accessory Checklist

Tele-adaptor   Y/N   Cost _____
Wide angle adapter Y/N   Cost _____
Extra batteries   Y/N   Cost _____
UV filter   Cost _____
Circular polarizing filter   Cost _____
Carrying case   Cost _____
Extra media   Cost _____
Other:_____   Cost _____
_____   Cost _____
_____   Cost _____
_____   Cost _____

POSTSCRIPT

It's time to say goodbye.

Whether your film is a feature film, or a family video, I hope that you capture extraordinary images.

My objective with this book has been to save you time, money and frustration. Hopefully I've helped you avoid some of the mistakes that I made, and made your life a little brighter.

I hope that you find the perfect camera for your uses, and that you make some wonderful digital video.

Good luck, and remember, "Keep shooting."

Tony Levelle
Lower Lake, California

ABOUT THE AUTHOR

Inspired by such available-light and low-budget films as Robert Rodriguez's *El Mariachi* and Jon Jost's *Frameup*, filmmaker Tony Levelle set out on a mission to learn how to do the same.

He had the good fortune to attend a seminar by Dorothy Fadiman who not only finished all the films she started and got every film into distribution, but kept them there!

He eventually worked with Fadiman and his co-authored book—*Producing with Passion: Making Films That Change the World*—is the result of their collaboration to share these techniques with others.

The quality of this book so impressed the publisher that even before it was finished they signed Tony to solo author *Digital Video Secrets: What the Pros Know and The Manuals Don't Tell You*.

Tony exemplifies the qualities all filmmakers need to survive: passion, persistence and vision.

Tony's website is www.tonylevelle.com. Visit his website for free *Digital Video Secrets* extras and recent news about digital video.

FILM DIRECTING: SHOT BY SHOT

VISUALIZING FROM CONCEPT TO SCREEN

STEVEN D. KATZ

BEST SELLER
OVER 190,000 COPIES SOLD!

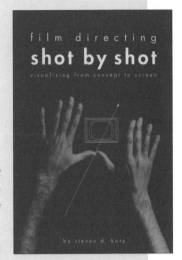

Film Directing: Shot by Shot — with its famous blue cover — is the best-known book on directing and a favorite of professional directors as an on-set quick reference guide.

This international bestseller is a complete catalog of visual techniques and their stylistic implications, enabling working filmmakers to expand their knowledge.

Contains in-depth information on shot composition, staging sequences, visualization tools, framing and composition techniques, camera movement, blocking tracking shots, script analysis, and much more.

Includes over 750 storyboards and illustrations, with never-before-published storyboards from Steven Spielberg's *Empire of the Sun*, Orson Welles' *Citizen Kane*, and Alfred Hitchcock's *The Birds*.

"(To become a director) you have to teach yourself what makes movies good and what makes them bad. John Singleton has been my mentor... he's the one who told me what movies to watch and to read Shot by Shot."
        – Ice Cube, *New York Times*

"A generous number of photos and superb illustrations accompany each concept, many of the graphics being from Katz' own pen... Film Directing: Shot by Shot is a feast for the eyes."
        – Videomaker Magazine

"... demonstrates the visual techniques of filmmaking by defining the process whereby the director converts storyboards into photographed scenes."
        – Back Stage Shoot

"Contains an encyclopedic wealth of information."
        – Millimeter Magazine

STEVEN D. KATZ is also the author of *Film Directing: Cinematic Motion*.

$27.95 · 366 PAGES · ORDER NUMBER 7RLS · ISBN: 0-941188-10-8

SETTING UP YOUR SHOTS
GREAT CAMERA MOVES EVERY FILMMAKER SHOULD KNOW

JEREMY VINEYARD

BEST SELLER
OVER 37,000 COPIES SOLD!

Written in straightforward, non-technical language and laid out in a nonlinear format with self-contained chapters for quick, on-the-set reference, *Setting Up Your Shots* is like a Swiss army knife for filmmakers! Using examples from over 140 popular films, this book provides detailed descriptions of more than 100 camera setups, angles, and techniques — in an easy-to-use horizontal "wide-screen" format.

Setting Up Your Shots is an excellent primer for beginning filmmakers and students of film theory, as well as a handy guide for working filmmakers. If you are a director, a storyboard artist, or an animator, use this book. It is the culmination of hundreds of hours of research.

Contains 150 references to the great shots from your favorite films, including *2001: A Space Odyssey*, *Blue Velvet*, *The Matrix*, *The Usual Suspects*, and *Vertigo*.

"*Perfect for any film enthusiast looking for the secrets behind creating film. Because of its simplicity of design and straightforward storyboards,* Setting Up Your Shots *is destined to be mandatory reading at film schools throughout the world.*"
        – Ross Otterman, *Directed By* Magazine

"Setting Up Your Shots *is a great book for defining the shots of today. The storyboard examples on every page make it a valuable reference book for directors and DPs alike! This great learning tool should be a boon for writers who want to choose the most effective shot and clearly show it in their boards for the maximum impact.*"
        – Paul Clatworthy, Creator, StoryBoard Artist and StoryBoard Quick Software

"*This book is for both beginning and experienced filmmakers. It's a great reference tool, a quick reminder of the most commonly used shots by the greatest filmmakers of all time.*"
        – Cory Williams, President, Alternative Productions

JEREMY VINEYARD is a filmmaker, internationally published author, and screenwriter. He is currently assembling a cast and crew for a crime feature.

$19.95 · 132 PAGES · ORDER NUMBER 8RLS · ISBN: 0-941188-73-6

24 HOURS | 1.800.833.5738 | WWW.MWP.COM

THE WRITER'S JOURNEY
3RD EDITION

MYTHIC STRUCTURE FOR WRITERS

CHRISTOPHER VOGLER

BEST SELLER
OVER 170,000 COPIES SOLD!

See why this book has become an international best seller and a true classic. *The Writer's Journey* explores the powerful relationship between mythology and storytelling in a clear, concise style that's made it required reading for movie executives, screenwriters, playwrights, scholars, and fans of pop culture all over the world.

Both fiction and nonfiction writers will discover a set of useful myth-inspired storytelling paradigms (i.e., "The Hero's Journey") and step-by-step guidelines to plot and character development. Based on the work of Joseph Campbell, *The Writer's Journey* is a must for all writers interested in further developing their craft.

The updated and revised third edition provides new insights and observations from Vogler's ongoing work on mythology's influence on stories, movies, and man himself.

"This book is like having the smartest person in the story meeting come home with you and whisper what to do in your ear as you write a screenplay. Insight for insight, step for step, Chris Vogler takes us through the process of connecting theme to story and making a script come alive."
> – Lynda Obst, Producer, *Sleepless in Seattle, How to Lose a Guy in 10 Days;* Author, *Hello, He Lied*

"This is a book about the stories we write, and perhaps more importantly, the stories we live. It is the most influential work I have yet encountered on the art, nature, and the very purpose of storytelling."
> – Bruce Joel Rubin, Screenwriter, *Stuart Little 2, Deep Impact, Ghost, Jacob's Ladder*

CHRISTOPHER VOGLER is a veteran story consultant for major Hollywood film companies and a respected teacher of filmmakers and writers around the globe. He has influenced the stories of movies from *The Lion King* to *Fight Club* to *The Thin Red Line* and most recently wrote the first installment of *Ravenskull*, a Japanese-style manga or graphic novel. He is the executive producer of the feature film *P.S. Your Cat is Dead* and writer of the animated feature *Jester Till*.

$26.95 · 300 PAGES · ORDER NUMBER 76RLS · ISBN: 193290736x

SAVE THE CAT!

THE LAST BOOK ON SCREENWRITING YOU'LL EVER NEED

BLAKE SNYDER

BEST SELLER

He's made millions of dollars selling screenplays to Hollywood and now screenwriter Blake Snyder tells all. "Save the Cat" is just one of Snyder's many ironclad rules for making your ideas more marketable and your script more satisfying – and saleable, including:

- The four elements of every winning logline.
- The seven immutable laws of screenplay physics.
- The 10 genres and why they're important to your movie.
- Why your Hero must serve your Idea.
- Mastering the Beats.
- Mastering the Board to create the Perfect Beast.
- How to get back on track with ironclad and proven rules for script repair.

This ultimate insider's guide reveals the secrets that none dare admit, told by a show biz veteran who's proven that you can sell your script if you can save the cat.

"Imagine what would happen in a town where more writers approached screenwriting the way Blake suggests? My weekend read would dramatically improve, both in sellable/producible content and in discovering new writers who understand the craft of storytelling and can be hired on assignment for ideas we already have in house."
> – From the Foreword by Sheila Hanahan Taylor, Vice President,
> Development at Zide/Perry Entertainment, whose films
> include *American Pie, Cats and Dogs* and *Final Destination*

"Want to know how to be a successful writer in Hollywood? The answers are here. Blake Snyder has written an insider's book that's informative – and funny, too."
> – David Hoberman, Producer, *Raising Helen, Walking Tall,*
> *Bringing Down the House*

"Blake Snyder's Save the Cat! *could also be called* Save the Screenwriter!*, because that's exactly what it will do:* Save the Screenwriter *time,* Save the Screenwriter *frustration, and* Save the Screenwriter's *sanity... by demystifying the Hollywood process."*
> – Andy Cohen, Literary Manager/Producer; President, Grade A Entertainment

BLAKE SNYDER has sold dozens of scripts, including co-writing the Disney hit, *Blank Check*, and *Nuclear Family* for Steven Spielberg – both million-dollar sales.

$19.95 · 216 PAGES · ORDER NUMBER 34RLS · ISBN: 1932907009

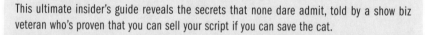

CINEMATIC STORYTELLING

THE 100 MOST POWERFUL FILM CONVENTIONS EVERY FILMMAKER MUST KNOW

JENNIFER VAN SIJLL

BEST SELLER

How do directors use screen direction to suggest conflict? How do screenwriters exploit film space to show change? How does editing style determine emotional response?

Many first-time writers and directors do not ask these questions. They forego the huge creative resource of the film medium, defaulting to dialog to tell their screen story. Yet most movies are carried by sound and picture. The industry's most successful writers and directors have mastered the cinematic conventions specific to the medium. They have harnessed non-dialog techniques to create some of the most cinematic moments in movie history.

This book is intended to help writers and directors more fully exploit the medium's inherent storytelling devices. It contains 100 non-dialog techniques that have been used by the industry's top writers and directors. From *Metropolis* and *Citizen Kane* to *Dead Man* and *Kill Bill*, the book illustrates — through 500 frame grabs and 75 script excerpts — how the inherent storytelling devices specific to film were exploited.

You will learn:
- How non-dialog film techniques can advance story.
- How master screenwriters exploit cinematic conventions to create powerful scenarios.

"Cinematic Storytelling scores a direct hit in terms of concise information and perfectly chosen visuals, and it also searches out... and finds... an emotional core that many books of this nature either miss or are afraid of."
> — Kirsten Sheridan, Director, *Disco Pigs*; Co-writer, *In America*

"Here is a uniquely fresh, accessible, and truly original contribution to the field. Jennifer van Sijl takes her readers in a wholly new direction, integrating aspects of screenwriting with all the film crafts in a way I've never before seen. It is essential reading not only for screenwriters but also for filmmakers of every stripe."
> — Prof. Richard Walter, UCLA Screenwriting Chairman

JENNIFER VAN SIJLL has taught film production, film history, and screenwriting. She is currently on the faculty at San Francisco State's Department of Cinema.

$24.95 · 230 PAGES · ORDER # 35RLS · ISBN: 193290705X

THE HOLLYWOOD STANDARD

THE COMPLETE AND AUTHORITATIVE GUIDE TO SCRIPT FORMAT AND STYLE

CHRISTOPHER RILEY

BEST SELLER

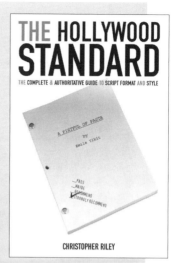

Finally, there's a script format guide that is accurate, complete, and easy to use, written by Hollywood's foremost authority on industry standard script formats. Riley's guide is filled with clear, concise, complete instructions and hundreds of examples to take the guesswork out of a multitude of formatting questions that perplex screenwriters, waste their time, and steal their confidence. You'll learn how to get into and out of a POV shot, how to set up a telephone intercut, what to capitalize and why, how to control pacing with format, and more.

"The Hollywood Standard *is not only indispensable, it's practical, readable, and fun to use.*"
— Dean Batali, Writer-Producer, *That '70s Show*; Writer, *Buffy the Vampire Slayer*

"*Buy this book before you write another word! It's required reading for any screenwriter who wants to be taken seriously by Hollywood.*"
— Elizabeth Stephen, President, Mandalay Television Pictures;
Executive Vice President Motion Picture Production, Mandalay Pictures

"*Riley has succeeded in an extremely difficult task: He has produced a guide to screenplay formatting which is both entertaining to read and exceptionally thorough. Riley's clear style, authoritative voice, and well-written examples make this book far more enjoyable than any formatting guide has a right to be. This is the best guide to script formatting ever, and it is an indispensable tool for every writer working in Hollywood.*"
— Wout Thielemans, *Screentalk* Magazine

"*It doesn't matter how great your screenplay is if it looks all wrong. The Hollywood Standard is probably the most critical book any screenwriter who is serious about being taken seriously can own. For any writer who truly understands the power of making a good first impression, this comprehensive guide to format and style is priceless.*"
— Marie Jones, www.absolutewrite.com

CHRISTOPHER RILEY, based in Los Angeles, developed Warner Brothers Studios script software and serves as the ultimate arbiter of script format for the entertainment industry.

$18.95 · 208 PAGES · ORDER # 31RLS · ISBN: 9781932907018

SAVE THE CAT! GOES TO THE MOVIES

THE SCREENWRITER'S GUIDE TO EVERY STORY EVER TOLD

BLAKE SNYDER

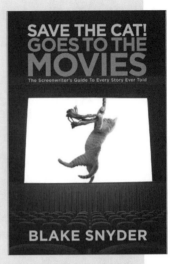

In the long-awaited sequel to his surprise bestseller, *Save the Cat!*, author and screenwriter Blake Snyder returns to form in a fast-paced follow-up that proves why his is the most talked-about approach to screenwriting in years. In the perfect companion piece to his first book, Snyder delivers even more insider's information gleaned from a 20-year track record as "one of Hollywood's most successful spec screenwriters," giving you the clues to write *your* movie.

Designed for screenwriters, novelists, and movie fans, this book gives readers the key breakdowns of the 50 most instructional movies from the past 30 years. From *M*A*S*H* to *Crash*, from *Alien* to *Saw*, from *10* to *Eternal Sunshine of the Spotless Mind*, Snyder reveals how screenwriters who came before you tackled the same challenges you are facing with the film you want to write — or the one you are currently working on.

Writing a "rom-com"? Check out the "Buddy Love" chapter for a "beat for beat" dissection of *When Harry Met Sally...* plus references to 10 other great romantic comedies that will make your story sing.

Want to execute a great mystery? Go to the "Whydunit" section and learn about the "dark turn" that's essential to the heroes of *All the President's Men*, *Blade Runner*, *Fargo* and hip noir *Brick* — and see why ALL good stories, whether a Hollywood blockbuster or a Sundance award winner, follow the same rules of structure outlined in Snyder's breakthrough method.

If you want to sell your script and create a movie that pleases most audiences most of the time, the odds increase if you reference Snyder's checklists and see what makes 50 films tick. After all, both executives and audiences respond to the same elements good writers seek to master. They want to know the type of story they signed on for, and whether it's structured in a way that satisfies everyone. It's what they're looking for. And now, it's what you can deliver.

BLAKE SNYDER, besides selling million-dollar scripts to both Disney and Spielberg, is still "one of Hollywood's most successful spec screenwriters," having made another spec sale in 2006. An in-demand scriptcoach and seminar and workshop leader, Snyder provides information for writers through his website, *www.blakesnyder.com*.

$22.95 · 270 PAGES · ORDER NUMBER 75RLS · ISBN: 1932907351

MICHAEL WIESE PRODUCTIONS

Our books are all about helping you create memorable films that will move audiences for generations to come.

Since 1981, we've published over 100 books on all aspects of filmmaking which are used in more than 600 film schools around the world. Many of today's most productive filmmakers and writers got started with our books.

According to a recent Nielsen BookScan analysis, as a publisher we've had more best-selling books in our subject category than our closest competitor — and they are backed by a multi-billion dollar corporation! This is evidence that as an independent — filmmaker or publisher — you can create the projects you have always dreamed of and earn a livelihood.

To help you accomplish your goals, we've expanded our information to the web. Here you can receive a 25% discount on all our books, buy the newest releases before they hit the bookstores, and sign up for a newsletter which provides all kinds of new information, tips, seminars, and more. You'll also find a Virtual Film School loaded with articles and websites from our top authors, teacher's guides, video streamed content, free budget formats, and a ton of free valuable information.

We encourage you to visit www.mwp.com. Sign up and become part of a wider creative community.

Onward and upward,
Michael Wiese
Publisher, Filmmaker

If you'd like to receive a free MWP Newsletter,
click on www.mwp.com to register.